RELUCTANTLY

Reluctantly

HAYDEN CARRUTH

Autobiographical Essays

 COPPER CANYON PRESS

The publication of this book was supported by grants from the Lannan Foundation, the Washington State Arts Commission, and by contributions from Elliott Bay Book Company, James Laughlin, and the members of the Friends of Copper Canyon Press. Copper Canyon Press is in residence with Centrum at Fort Worden State Park.

"Fragments of Autobiography: First Series" and "Suicide" previously appeared in *Suicides and Jazzers* (The University of Michigan Press, 1993). Reprinted by permission.

Library of Congress Cataloging-in-Publication Data

Carruth, Hayden, 1921–
  Reluctantly: autobiographical essays / by Hayden Carruth. – 1st ed.
  p. cm.

  ISBN 1-55659-089-X
  1. Carruth, Hayden, 1921– Biography. 2. Poets, American – 20th century –
Biography. I. Title.
  PS3505.A77594 Z477 1998
  811'.54 – DDC21
  [B]

                                98-19742
                                  CIP

9 8 7 6 5 4 3 2 FIRST EDITION

COPPER CANYON PRESS
P.O. BOX 271, PORT TOWNSEND, WA 98368

Contents

IV Preface

 1 Fragments of Autobiography: First Series

41 Suicide

69 Footnote to Suicide

71 Fragments of Autobiography: Second Series

165 About the Author

Preface

PEOPLE HAVE ASKED ME when the pieces in this book were written, but I can't help them, at least not much. I don't keep good enough records. All I know for certain is that the essay on suicide was written in 1988. The autobiographical fragments in the first series were written before then, I think, and those in the second series after. The earliest date from twenty-five years ago or more. The latest are from 1995 and 1996.

It's an utterly miscellaneous book, in other words. A number of times I've been asked to write a proper autobiography, a tight narrative with the usual dovetails, diagrams, and genealogical apparatus. No, I've said. How can I write like that about myself when so much of myself has been constructed by others, those for whom I cannot and would not speak?

People have also asked about the title. Can anyone publish something reluctantly? Either you publish or you don't, isn't that right? Well, I can't answer this either, although I believe an answer, a complicated, tenuous one, exists somewhere in the depths, if one had sufficient patience and ingenuity to seek it out. Superficially speaking, I *am* reluctant. But friends and relations have persuaded me to suppress my feeling.

A better title might be: *O Manitou, God of Our Little Lost Indians Everywhere, What the Fuck Is the Meaning of It All?*

H.C.

MUNNSVILLE

APRIL 11, 1998

RELUCTANTLY

Fragments of Autobiography: First Series

SOMEWHERE NEAR Villeneuve de Berg in the Ardèche is a hill I visited a number of times when I lived briefly in that region ten years ago. Not a knoll or a cobble, but a good-sized hill, part of the system of foothills leading northwestward to the Massif Central. I don't remember its name.

At the base of the hill was a scattering of homes, the farthest fringe of the village, some of them old farmhouses, others more recently built. Gardens, cars, children's toys; the usual pleasant clutter. Farther up the slope were terraced orchards, mostly of polled mulberry trees, gnarled and ancient, with overgrown scrub oak, vines, and tall grasses; a grazing place for goats. A small broken-down *magnanerie* in a gully was evidence of the silk culture that had helped sustain the upland country of the Midi in the time before synthesized fabrics. The whole hill was strewn with jagged boulders of limestone, glacial detritus. Small hand-lettered wooden signs, the letters carved or charred, marked the boundaries of truffle-hunting grounds to which local people hold hereditary rights, not necessarily coinciding with other property lines, which causes, at least in my mind, a certain agreeable confusion.

At the top of the hill was a ruined village from the eighteenth century and earlier. Lines of sprawling, pale, angular stones marked the walls of buildings whose timbered parts had long since rotted away; longer lines marked a principal street and two or three secondary ones. There were larger rectangles too, which I took to be pens and corrals. It must have been a village inhabited by shepherds, perhaps only in summer.

Elsewhere indications of a still earlier culture remained. Toward its far end the village dispersed completely into rubble, reminding me of Old Oraibe and other ancient pueblos of the southwest. I found there fields of stone so dense that hardly any vegetation could grow, nothing but a few stunted junipers and oaks. At one place archaeologists had cleared the site of an Aurignacian dolmen, an impressive structure of huge flattish stones, three to form the walls and a fourth, still larger, laid over the top for a roof, what the French call *une table*. I believe the site of a menhir was also on that hill, though I may be confusing it with another I saw; menhirs, the upright columns we associate with Stonehenge, are less common than dolmens in southern France. When I walked farther, stepping from stone to stone – in this I had a certain skill from walking in my brook in Vermont – I found another dolmen, partly fallen, its site uncleared, and also the entrance to a cave, a black opening, two or three feet wide, down into the earth, so ringed by white, jagged stones that it could he called toothy. I nearly fell into it, but made no attempt to descend, being not partial to caves. Was it a big cave? Did it have paintings on its walls? Almost certainly not. The hole showed no sign of activity by scholars or tourists. My knowledge of archaeology and geology was – and is – slight. Did the Stone Age people live on top of that hill? At any rate they did *something* up there; no mistake about that.

Then there were the moonfaces, as I called them, which I saw many times in that region, perfectly round, carved in half-relief on lintels, end-stones, herms, etc. I could learn nothing about them from the local people, but I presumed they were originally Celtic and late neolithic, a culture which in those hills might have lasted well into Roman times. Surrounded by all that history I felt my ignorance keenly. "Go read some books," I told myself.

But ruins were everywhere in that poor, devastated region. The village I lived in, Lagorce, which was a little farther south, was eighty percent destroyed. All that remained of the old chateau were a few broken walls, a half-buried room, and signs of a moat. Many houses in the village were only broken walls. Most of the inhabitants were old people, or outsiders like myself.

Well, in a desultory way I did read a few books, mostly about the history and language of Occitania, but I am not a scholar. My curiosity, alas, is not the kind that can be satisfied by objective knowledge. Plato said that opinion is worthless and that only knowledge counts, which is a neat formulation, attractive to Mediterranean temperaments, including Yeats's (e.g., in "A Prayer for My Daughter"). But melancholy Danes from the northern mists understand that opinion is all there is. The great questions transcend fact, and discourse is a process of personality. Knowledge cannot respond to knowledge. And wisdom? Is it not opinion refined, opinion killed and resuscitated upward? Maybe Plato would have agreed with this.

I liked to sit in a particular spot at the top of that hill near Villeneuve de Berg, on a wall of the ruined village, looking out toward the terraced slopes of other hills in the distance. Over my shoulder I could see the dolmen in its mute significance, could almost see the ancient folk struggling to raise and move those stones weighing many tons. All about me lay the silent remains of a village that had once, to judge by the number and complexity of its walls, been a bustling community. Both inside and outside the village were shallow diggings, evidence that hunters of wild truffles were still at work, though surely theirs is a dying trade. Down below was the silk culture, already quite dead. A few miles farther into the Massif I had seen beautiful chestnut orchards and the villages, now poor as dirt, of the people who in past centuries had invented scores of ways to use the hulls, shells, and meats of *le marron* and had lived on their inventions. A few miles away in Largentière I could still overhear women gossiping in *lo lenga doc* in the churchyard of what had once been an Albigensian cathedral. Thousands upon thousands of ghosts whispered in the air around me; many layers and levels of culture. Even the living were assimilated, a sound of hammering and radio music from the foot of the hill, a jet overhead signing the blue sky with its contrail. The earth itself, the stony wreckage and rickety vegetation, was as clear in its significance as any slaughtering ground. Every natural thing is transitory and contained in its own nonexistence. Every species, the human as well as the rest, is extinct. Why? What for?

I was reminded of the time many years earlier when my family had spent part of each summer at the place of a close friend in the remote countryside of Dutchess County, New York. This was in the twenties and early thirties. The town, named Dover Furnace after the old stone smelteries still to be seen there, which were said to have furnished iron for Revolutionary cannon, at that time had a railway station, store, and post office, now disappeared. Electric power was unavailable, so our friend had built a sizable dam, twenty-five feet high, across a stream on his property and had installed his own generator and transmission lines. I was a boy of eight or nine. The spot where I liked to sit then was on top of that dam between two spillways which controlled the flow of water and the level of the millpond; in other words I liked the roar of water in my ears, which effectively shut me off from the rest of the universe. It was a point of stillness, so to speak, in the immensity of action. The blade of grass being twitched by the current on the bank of the stream below me, the oriole flying across my field of vision to its nest in an elm a hundred feet beyond, were motions seeming vastly distant as I sat in the roar of eternity on either side. I was truly isolated. And what I thought about was: Why? What for?

The purposelessness of it all, of existence as such, had struck me at so early an age that I have no idea when it happened or how. Perhaps it came from a conjunction of my father's atheism and my mother's conventional Episcopalian faith. (I went to Sunday school because the other kids did. It seemed to me a strange place.) Or perhaps it came from some early, repressed encounter with personal death. More likely it was the result of many causes, too lost to be known. But I had always been aware that the Universe is sad; everything in it, animate or inanimate, the wild creatures, the stones, the stars, was enveloped in the great sadness, pervaded by it. Existence had no use. It was without end or reason. The most beautiful things in it, a flower or a song, as well as the most compelling, a desire or a thought, were pointless. So great a sorrow. And I knew that the only rest from my anxiety – for I had been trembling even in infancy – lay in acknowledging and absorbing this sadness, as I did when I sat on top of the dam, a boy at the deafening instant between the future and the past.

Never then or now have I been able to look at a cloudless sky at night and see beauty there. A kind of grandeur, yes – but not beauty. The profusion and variety of celestial lights have always frightened me. Why are they there? Why these instead of others? Why these instead of nothing? And no received faith or reason has ever helped me one iota in answering.

What is the difference between a "natural object" and a "man-made object?" None. In ultimate terms – and I've never been able to think otherwise than ultimately; no wonder my scholarship is paltry – all things in reality are part of reality, and hence are equal; they all plunge equally into transitoriness and nonexistence. The only meaning, such as men and women pretend to find in mathematical or poetic statements, is the meaning of obliteration. The only absolute value is value itself inverted, turned inside out – the void. And long before I came intellectually to the realization that the notion of relative value implies inescapably a hierarchical structure, which thus tends toward illegitimate triadism, dualism, monism – and it wasn't easy to give up my pragmatic Yankee view, my agreeable fondness for Mr. Peirce and W. James – I knew that everything is equivalent, every pebble and masterpiece, every atom and thought of love: they are *precisely* the same in value. The idea of value is an invention – at its best a sick joke and at its worst an inexpressible sorrow. Many times in the past twenty-five years I have been called a "nature poet." I'm grateful to anyone who takes the trouble to read something I have written, of course, but wish to say also, quietly but insistently, that if I am a nature poet, then the understanding of nature which I have suggested here is fundamental to my work; it is, literally, the foundation. I think it can be seen in most of my poems, except that readers are predisposed to overlook it. Naturally, like most people, I am prone to changes of mood; at any given time (but aren't they all "given?") my cheerfulness in the face of existence may be more or, usually, less than at other times. But at all times my perception of what exists, the whole or a part, is of the absence of intelligence, except for the weak, insipid, tedious, petulant, and inadequate intelligence of human beings. But to say this merely on my own behalf would not be enough to justify writing it here. I believe I speak for a good many others. Elsewhere I have explained my aversion to the lovelessness, arrogance, and egomania of Henry D. Thoreau in his book called *Walden*.[1] I won't recapitulate the argument here. But it is worth noting that many readers, though five women for every man, have told me that they understand my view and share it. They see the connection between Thoreau's so-called Transcendentalism, i.e., his flight from reality, and the violence and irresponsibility of the American frontier, which are now in a fair way to becoming the national way of life. My view is not extreme; on the contrary it is a middle ground between Thoreau's expropriative, solipsistic vision of nature and the systematic disdain we find, for instance, in the work of a European like Jean-Paul Sartre. Yet Americans have been so brainwashed by continual subjection to *Walden* that my moderative tendencies seem actually out of line. It isn't that when you pick up the book review section of the Sunday *New York Times* you will find that easily half the reviews emit a Waldenesque smell; it is rather that a great number of those who are reading the reviews will, once they put down the paper, go out on Sunday birdwalks with all of *Walden*'s snobbery and righteousness and sentimentalism crammed in their heads. I believe no other book in English has been more widely read by the American middle class, by millions and millions of comparatively well-heeled and powerful people. It is a touchstone even for those who work with nature – scientists, forestry professors, veterinarians, state fish and game administrators, and so on. The one class of country people who have not read it is the farmers and farm

---

[1] "The Man in the Box at Walden," *Selected Essays and Reviews*, Copper Canyon Press, 1996.

workers, though they too have been affected by it from a distance and derivatively. *Everyone* had been affected – and infected. We need a national antitoxin.

That's what a small band of us is trying to provide. We are profoundly attached to nature, our lives are dominated by it and we write about it, we write about flowers, birds, the differing intensities of color in autumn, the venation of a locust's wing, about the greatest manifestations and the least (which are, in fact, equivalencies), but we do so clear-sightedly. To the mass of the literati we say: Have the kindness to understand what we are trying to do, what we are actually writing, before you make pronouncements about it. (The "favorable" pronouncements are often as silly as their opposites.) Cling to your Thoreauvian TV if you must, to Walt Disney and John Wayne – those twins! – to the National Geographic and *Miami Vice*. But please refrain from criticizing us in ignorance. Our number is small, but it is growing, and we have young, vigorous leaders, people like Audre Lorde, George Dennison, John Ashbery, Grace Paley, Cid Corman, June Jordan, Leo Connellan, Ray Carver, Edward Hoagland, and others, as well as some though not all of the essayists who write about specific matters of environmental understanding in the pop magazines, people as diverse in style and temperament as any you could choose; but they are clear-sighted. They know what the earth is and what it means. If we are to find a way to proceed beyond the violence that is crippling us now in every sphere, beyond the egomaniacal sentimentality that cripples us just as much, the main intention of these people and others like them must prevail.

A NUMBER OF WOMEN of my generation or earlier have told me that they were knowledgeable about the facts of sex and reproduction when they were children – five or six years old, say – but that they then repressed this knowledge so completely that later, when they were adolescent and necessity required them to rediscover these facts, they suffered an emotional trauma. This was an aspect of the general difficulty women have always had, but especially during the Victorian age, as it is called, and the time while the influence of that age continued in American civilization – as in some respects it continues even now – an aspect, but only one, of the difficulty women have experienced in growing up in a sexist society. Probably in our so-called open society today most young girls are spared this kind of repression and trauma. Which is an important topic, but not what I want to write about here. Instead I want to say that I understand clearly how such strange repression and trauma can occur, though most young people today would find it unimaginable, because I experienced the same things with respect to my knowledge of personal death.

When does a child become aware of personal death? Some psychiatrists argue that for infants the experience of birth itself may be an experience of death, of the destruction of reality, which I have no trouble accepting. At the very least it must be an experience of radical vulnerability. But it occurs so early that we cannot consciously remember the happening of it; we think we were born with it. Thus I can't tell when my knowledge of personal death first came to me, but I do know from certain corroborative thoughts and images that if I did not have it "always," I had it well before the age of three, when my family moved from Waterbury to Woodbury in Connecticut. I know further that it was associated with the person of my father, the stranger who waited for me outside the womb. What I cannot know – one of the billions of things – is how long it took me to move from my virtually instantaneous knowledge of my own death to the inference that he, the stranger, would also die, and would die before me.

All our lives we are the accomplices of Time, our mortal enemy. It is the treason against ourselves that we cannot resist. What twists of mind we are left with as a result!

Though they are there in my mind, these memories are shadowy. But the fact of repression is not. Of course I don't mean I completely repressed the facts of life and death, which would be impossible. But their urgency, their immediate and felt relationship to my personal existence, their enormous capacity to frighten me – these were "forgotten." And my parents did everything they could to abet this. One of the events of my childhood that now seems perhaps the most extraordinary of all was when I was told of my grandmother's – my father's mother's – death. This was when I was eight or nine years old. I had known her well. Although she and my grandfather lived more than fifty miles away – a real journey in the twenties; by car, when we were lucky enough to have the use of one, it took three or four hours, and by train more than that as well as a considerable wait to make a connection at Brewster – I saw them often on holidays and in the summer. I knew my grandmother as a kindly old lady with gray hair who wore shapeless dresses and black, lace-up shoes, a woman who was recessive in her household, did not talk much, spent her time baking pies and frying doughnuts, but who was friendly and welcoming and imaginative in her relationships with children. She paid attention to me. She told me stories and thought of things for me to do. When I was told of her death, I grieved. But not deeply nor long, because my grief was dispelled almost immediately by a sense of mystery operating on many levels.

I was told of her death not only after she died but after her funeral and burial. Yet she had died in our house. She had lived in our house for some time before her death, I don't remember how long, perhaps a couple of months, bedridden with cancer, cared for by my mother and father and hired nurses. Our house was not a mansion by any means; it was a poor man's house with seven small rooms. Yet I never saw my grandmother in her final illness, I was not permitted to go into her room. I was unaware of her death, I was unaware of the removal of her body, I had never even heard any suspicious noises, and the whole episode was kept from me until after her funeral by what must have been an almost inconceivably elaborate subterfuge, in which my grandmother herself, in her final suffering, must have concurred.

That was Victorianism. Death was taboo in our house. So was sex. These topics were never mentioned. I don't mean that they were casually omitted in a mutually acknowledged understanding, such as one can find in many homes today; probably in almost any home some topic – the father's birthmark, the mother's addiction to soap opera – will be unmentionable. But in our home death and sex were so systematically ignored that they could not exist. Our mutually acknowledged understanding was that if either of these topics were spoken of, some great catastrophe would ensue, reality would be shattered. When I was much older, in my midthirties, living for a few years with my parents because I was acutely ill and had nowhere else to go, the three of us were playing Scrabble one night – a game I soon despised – and I made the word *venery*. "What does that mean?" my mother asked. I had uttered only the first fragment of a speech-sound in response when my father, blushing beet red, broke in, "It means the art of hunting deer." Later I looked it up in the unabridged dictionary, and by God he was right – as he was so often when it came to questions of language: I had plenty of occasion to marvel at his vocabulary. The "art of hunting deer" is a secondary meaning. But here was my mother, a woman in her fifties who had been married for years and had borne three children, yet who, in America and in the fifties, could still not be "subjected" to a largely archaic and in a sense technical, respectable term that in its primary meaning signifies fucking or sexual lust in general. (Etymologically they are two separate words, both spelled *venery*.) This is the degree of repression my father suffered from all his life, which he imposed on the rest of his family. What it meant was a peculiar shallowness in the quality of family experience, which I think was common in lower-middle-class English homes during the Victorian and Edwardian periods, and in American homes that imitated them, resulting in all kinds of trivial and disguised and absurdly unnatural behavior.

Children were "Brownies," who lived forever. Sprites and fairies inhabited the woods. Santa Claus was the intimate friend not only of small children but of adults. The extent of such fancies is nearly unbelievable now. I had to pretend a belief in Santa Claus long beyond the time when I had been disillusioned, even until I was twelve or thirteen years old; in fact we never came to an open agreement that Father Christmas was a fantasy. The adult family was almost as deeply trapped in what my father might have called – if he had known the jargon of criticism – "necessary fictions," as the family of children had been.

All this was accomplished without resort to a religious base. My father had seen angels – so he said – but at the same time he was a proclaimed atheist. My mother's efforts to give me and my younger brothers at least some grounding in low church Episcopalianism were smothered by my father's radical rationalism. Of course I did not discover until long afterward that this combination of rationalism and materialism with fantasized spirituality was deeply rooted in English Romanticism and post-Romanticism, from Shelley to Morris to Swinburne, and that my father, past the middle of the twentieth century, was still living in a watered-down pre-Raphaelitish, Blakean (as in *Songs of Innocence* – his favorite poem was the first one in that book), and *Yellow-Book*-like era. A spiritual element existed in our life, in other words, but it had no footing in the real cultural and historical place of the family, and hence was perceived by the children as tenuous and even anomalous.

Two books that were imposed on me when I was a child were *Alice in Wonderland* and Charles Kingsley's *Water Babies*. I loathed both of them. I knew this at the time and did everything I could not to be affected by them, even to the extent of hiding the books. (Destruction would have been unthinkable.) But only much later did I come to see that my loathing was a consequence of stifled fear, a profound mortal terror. To this day I cannot take pleasure in fantasy and have resisted such authors as Tolkien and C. S. Lewis.

As for the trauma, the necessary rediscovery, it came later in my adolescence than I would now have expected, and I don't know how to account for that. I was a freshman in college, seventeen years old. Perhaps this is substantiating evidence of the degree of repression I had undergone. I was a student at the University of North Carolina in Chapel Hill. I was living in a boarding house on the western edge of town, a large house with a pillared veranda next to a big magnolia tree, but it was a shabby house that badly needed painting and repair. This was in the depth of the Great Depression. The landlord was a peddler of cheap jewelry, a sharp dresser with a battered sample case who went from door to door in little towns, from farm to farm in the country. I remember once or twice when he sat with us, the students, in the evening; he would be brushing his thinning hair with an old silver-backed military hairbrush and telling us how this benefited the scalp and stimulated the growth of new hair. His wife was a drab woman. She was thin and had straight black hair that fell limply around her face, which looked ravaged by work and anxiety; she wore old dresses and sweaters with holes in their elbows. They lived in the back of the house, I think in what had originally been the servants' quarters, and I slept in a small room, not much more than a closet, where I could hear them through the wall. One night she asked him if they could make love. I can't remember her words. What I remember is her whispering, which nevertheless expressed urgency, and her gist was clear enough. "No," he said, "I don't want to, I'm too tired." From fucking all those farm women, I thought, after you've sold them pieces of trash for more money than they ought to spend. And then immediately I bolted upright, thinking: *I am going to die*. Not casually, not I'm gonna die someday like everyone else; but rather, I, this self, this focus of identity, all I have, all I am right now – *this* will be *annihilated, I* will become *extinct*. In my bed my eyes smarted, my heart thundered, my breath was labored as if my own throat were strangling me. Plenty of times before I had been afraid, and as I know now all my life from an early age had been governed by hidden anxiety, but this was different. It was terror, panic. I made no sound, I did nothing but lie down again and pull the covers over me, but I was out of control. I did not sleep that night. And to tell the truth, during most of the thousands of nights since then I haven't slept much either.

Why this happened on that particular night and at that particular moment is not hard to understand.

WOODBURY, THE TOWN in western Connecticut where I lived from age three to thirteen, stretched for several miles along its Main Street, which was – and still is – the old U.S. Route 6 that joins Provincetown, Massachusetts, to the West Coast. In the twenties it was an important highway; I thought living next to it was rather significant, though I couldn't have said of what. From our steps that led down the bank to the road, my friend Ralph and I watched the passing cars for hours, dozens and scores of different makes, which we could identify and upon whose qualities we held complex opinions: Dusenbergs, Stutzes, Pierce Arrows, Franklins (air-cooled cars with funny-looking hoods), Studebakers, Dodges, and so on, down to the lowly Model Ts that we called Tin Lizzies – when one went by we routinely hollered, "Get a horse!" Fairly often we saw cars with out-of-state markers, as we called the license plates; occasionally we saw a car from far away, from Florida, Colorado, or even California, and this was cause for rejoicing in our limited lives.

Like most towns in New England, Woodbury was extensive. Woodbury and North Woodbury, with perhaps three miles of Main Street between them, were the principal foci; they were fully independent and had their own post offices and town administrations. But the school district incorporated both. Other early settlements had been absorbed by the two towns but still were separate communities and had their own names, such as Pomperaug, Middle Quarter, Hotchkissville, the West Side, Sherman Hill, and so on, connected by many gravel roads and by the river and its system of tributary brooks. Other names were important too: the Green, the Dump, the Dam, the Blacksmith's, the Iron Bridge, the Indian Grave, the Quarry, the Cliff. This last was part of a granite ridge that lay parallel to Main Street and east of it. The Masonic Temple stood on top of the cliff, just at the point where the Indian maiden had jumped to her death in despair for her love of a white settler. Every town in New England, and for all I know in the rest of the country, has an Indian maiden in its mythology, and the meaning of these hapless women in American culture could not be charmingly extrapolated, I'm sure.

Farther back, on the highest point of the ridge, stood the Fire Tower. It was an open structure of steel girders and struts about eighty feet high with a railed wooden platform at the top, then a roof over the platform and a wooden pole rising from the center of the roof. I don't know what the pole was, perhaps a flagstaff or a support for a radio antenna, more likely just a decoration; the fact is that I never saw the fire tower manned. I suppose during times of drought the town or the state may have posted someone to keep watch, but I don't recall ever seeing anyone up there who looked like a fire-watcher, and the tower was clearly visible from Main Street. What I do recall is that every boy in Woodbury who was worth his salt had to have his initials carved in that pole, which was six-sided, not round. It meant climbing to the platform, standing on the rail, hoisting oneself out, up, and over the edge of the roof – eighty feet in the air – then hanging on with one hand and using one's jackknife with the other. And then, of course, getting back down. What folly for anyone. For a boy already afflicted with the acrophobia that would become pathologically extreme a few years later, it wasn't foolish, it was crazy. Nevertheless I did it.

No doubt by now if that tower still stands its pole is etched and over-etched with hundreds of initials. Which means that hundreds of boys have looked at that sloping roof in terror; they have looked death in the face and defied it. For what? Vanity. Yet perhaps it was not a bad thing for boys to do.

I was scared up there, and I remember my fear, but I remember also how beautiful the town looked from the tower, especially in the fall. Such an intensity of color – red, orange, yellow – rising from the woods and hills, from the great maples that lined the roads and shaded the houses. The October sky, brilliantly blue; the October air, its effervescent freshness. On a Saturday afternoon one could see from the tower scores of thin, blue columns of smoke rising from the town, spreading out at a certain elevation below the ridgelines of the hills. The townspeople were burning their leaves. In those days we felt no remissness if we burned the leaves instead of composting them, and the smoke with its piquant smell was no pollution. On the contrary it was a sign of seasonal change, of ritual change, always welcome. The labor of summer was over, the harvest completed, the cows were in the barn (or soon would be). It was a time to put on our worn flannel shirts and old woolen sweaters raveling at the elbows, so comfortable, conformable. In our family we wore old clothes from necessity, but with a kind of gratification too, derived in part from ordinary Yankee feelings of thrift, but in part also from something more indistinct and perhaps especially important to the Carruths – a knowledge that we were common folk and that the common values, including those of common suffering, were worth noticing.

Even during the affluent twenties, Woodbury was a poor town. No one was starving, though a few families lived on the edge of it, especially in winter, those pitiful families whose genetic resources in the back country had dwindled over centuries. (Woodbury was first settled in 1636.) Many of the farms were too small, stony, overworked, and infertile to be productive. Some of these, especially north of town, had been taken up by Lithuanian refugees, who were struggling to make a foothold in America. Their children, with unpronounceable, unspellable names, came to school in tattered clothes, the boys in drab vests and the girls in more colorful ones, both sexes with strange crude haircuts and their stockings falling down. The rest of us shunned them. Children are not just cruel, they are barbarous. But in truth, if it makes any difference, the strangeness of the Lithuanians, not their poverty, was what made them alien to us. How remote and isolated Woodbury was – no Italians, no Jews, no Portuguese. The one French-Canadian family, the St. Pierres, had been there for several generations; and the one black family, the Fords, had descended from northern slaves freed before the Revolution. No, the Lithuanians, three or four families, were our foreigners, whose children were called *snot-nosed* as a matter of course.

But not in October. Who could be xenophobic in the midst of that glory? Autumn was a time of good health and clear thinking, so it seemed to me. People died in winter, spring, summer, but not in autumn. Autumn was beautiful, fleeting, touched with the premonitory sorrow that I somehow came at an early age to recognize as the fundamental quality of all existence. The trees, the stones, the stars: all were consummately beautiful, and all were condemned to mutability.

Perhaps the best of autumn was to sit on the cool grass at the end of afternoon while the piles of leaves still smoldered and eat Concord grapes taken in ripe clusters from the vine, which sprawled on the arbor of cedar poles my father had made for it.

WHEN I BEGAN TO SMOKE in earnest I can't remember. It was well before I was thirteen, which is when my family moved from Woodbury to New York State. I know I experimented with tobacco when I was five or six, stealing from packs of Lucky Strikes my Uncle Max left lying around the house. I can remember sitting in the sun on the hill that sloped down from our back fence, out of sight from the house, lighting cigarettes and blowing the smoke out in gusty huffs, studying the way a cigarette looked in my hand. I can remember trying to chew a pinch of my father's pipe tobacco. By the age of nine I was picking up butts from the street, saving them in the fold at the waist of my sweater. My friend Ralph, who lived across the road and was a year younger than I, was a smoker too; we snagged butts and smoked them together in the loft of his family's barn, which was not used for storing hay, or in the woods. I can remember smoking in the icehouse that was near Sullivan's Pond. I can remember being taught to inhale smoke by an older boy when we were walking home from school, in a gravel pit off toward the eastern edge of town; he took a drag on his cigarette, opened his mouth to show me the smoke, then breathed it down into his lungs. He handed me the cigarette and I tried it. Of course it made me dizzy, but I pretended I didn't feel a thing. Which, ever since, is what I have pretended generally.

I remember buying cigarettes at the drugstore by saying they were for my uncle. I remember when the druggist, having been alerted by some busybody, told me I couldn't have any more. I remember sitting on the girder of the steel-truss bridge over the Pomperaug River, thirty feet above the swimming hole, with Margaret Shean, a freckled, sexy-looking, intelligent girl from my eighth-grade class at school, beside me. We were in bathing suits, as we called them then; I was smoking and had a pack of Camels in my hand. Margaret was Irish and Catholic – she went to my school because Woodbury had no parochial school – and a little prim, and she was nagging me in a covertly flirtatious way, which was the only kind of flirtation twelve-year-olds could imagine in 1932. "Why don't you throw those cigarettes away?" she said. I turned my hand over and dropped the pack down into the river. It floated away. What an unusual and romantic thing to do! – that's what I told myself, and Margaret put her hand on my wrist. I can bring back to my mind without effort the sensations of her touch and the gratification and excitement and mystery I felt as a consequence of what I had done. But I'm sure I had got my hands on some more cigarettes, one way or another, before the sun went down.

(Incidentally, the image of that pack of Camels falling toward the water, falling flat and without turning and hitting the water an instant later with a little splat, remains vivid in my mind for another reason. Why didn't I pitch myself after it and dash out my brains on the rocks below? At the time I don't believe I was tempted, but now, after fifty-five years of phobic, including acrophobic, conditioning, I am retrospectively – and powerfully – tempted. The vision, as vivid as anything in my memory, of that pack of cigarettes, which had been a part of myself, falling toward the water seems to draw me after it and makes me gasp every time I think of it. I suspect I've thought of it every day since it happened.)

I loved to watch people smoking. The farm boys at the diner could drag in such riches of smoke from their unfiltered Chesterfields and Old Golds that it came out in ropes and loops from their mouths and nostrils. The local businessmen would light up their Luckies by striking kitchen matches, which they kept in the side pockets of their suit coats, with their thumbnails, then blow out the match with a long straight plume of smoke. Another of my uncles, who talked loudly, would smoke his Camels in a paper holder with a goose-quill tip, like FDR's, and he would talk and exhale smoke at the same time, so that the smoke came out every which way, as if it were the ectoplasmic embodiment of his language. Mostly women didn't smoke in those days, but sometimes I saw a college girl from Vassar – in those years we often spent weekends at Dover Furnace, New York, not far from Poughkeepsie – who smoked or pretended to, dressed in a big sweater and short pleated skirt with her hair bobbed and a huge necklace swinging on her nearly breastless front. But such girls smoked effetely, holding the cigarette between thumb and index finger like a European, puffing the smoke out without inhaling it, batting their eyes. I scorned them. In the winter when my breath was visible I loved to blow out vapor as if it were smoke, using a twig or a pencil for a cigarette, and I studied the different shapes I could give my "smoke" by changing my mouth and the tilt of my head. In those years smoke meant more to me than marbles, hockey, my solitary reading and writing, or the glimpse of a girl's underwear when she was putting on her arctics, as we called overshoes. I was an addict before I had smoked five cartons of real cigarettes, five ounces of Prince Albert or Edgeworth. I was sold on smoke from the very beginning, the way some kids are sold on training for the Olympics or giving a recital in Town Hall at the age of thirteen.

Of course my family hated the idea of my smoking and rejected it absolutely. This was part of the whole mind-set of Carruthian secular and neurotic puritanism, as was the fear of talking about it, of talking about anything that might be charged with negative feeling. So the fiction was maintained for years, all during my adolescence, that I didn't smoke. I smoked out the window of my bedroom. I smoked when I went walking at night in the quiet side streets of Pleasantville. I smoked behind the school with my friends or at the swimming pool in summer. By the time I was fifteen I had been thoroughly shanghaied by both cigarettes and pipes, a condition my family at last acknowledged when I went to college a couple of years later. By the time I was twenty-five I was knowledgeable about the grades of Havana filler, binder, and wrapper, East Indian and African blends, cigars from Connecticut like Muniemachers, Kafkas, and Judges Caves, pipe tobaccos such as white burley, bright leaf, Cavendish, perique from Louisiana, Latakia, and Turkish and Macedonian varieties whose names I no longer remember. But mainly I smoked Camels, two or three packs a day. At age forty I gave up cigarettes and for about fifteen years smoked only pipes (twenty a day, mostly Granger Rough Cut) and cigars (two or three a day if I could afford them), and then gradually in my late fifties I succumbed to cigarettes again, though now the filtered, "low-tar" kinds. Today I smoke usually two packs of cigarettes a day, five pipes, and one or two cigars.

In other words I smoke all the time. Only rarely do I encounter a smoker like me. To smoke twenty pipes a day, as I did for years, one must live with a cindered mouth, a mouth no better than a charcoal brazier. To smoke as many cigarettes as I do one must cough continually, wheeze and pant, accept constant inflammation of lungs, throat, nose, etc. The pain is considerable. At night, when I go to bed after a day of smoking, I often have such pain in my chest, such difficulty with breathing, that I become truly frightened and dream about suffocation, the death I fear most. And of course everyone knows now, though we did not when I was young, about the hidden damages, cancer, emphysema, heart weakness, clogged arteries – the deaths that smoking brings to us, 370,000 a year in America. I am writing this on the twenty-fifth anniversary of the first Surgeon General's warning printed on cigarette packages; this news on the radio is what has impelled me to put such a wretched history into words. Now for twenty-five years I have been reading that forecast of my own death! And I believe my addiction is more profound today than it has ever been.

Every morning when I get up, no matter how rotten I've felt the night before, I reach for a cigarette automatically, and smoke five or six while I have my coffee. If I don't do this I begin immediately to feel a great psychic itch, untranslatable into any language, that prevents me from working or doing much of anything. I have no doubt whatever that this addiction is mostly "psychological"; it is in my head, and is so involved in my personality, like the innermost cog of a machine, that I am dysfunctional without it. The nicotine is unimportant. The symbolic and attitudinal significance of smoking is everything. My life depends on it.

A painter whom I particularly admire and whose work seems to me close to my own in poetry is Vlaminck, especially in his later paintings of French farms and villages. He was also a musician who played in clubs and dance halls and a competitive cyclist, a tough and independent guy. I have never seen a photo of him in which he wasn't smoking a cigarette, pipe, or cigar. He was a smoker like me. Maybe that's part of the reason for my attraction to his work, though certainly only a part. He was a damned good painter.

What is the reason for this addiction? Do I still get pleasure from smoking? Not much. Since the Cuban embargo, almost thirty years ago, I have never found a cigar I enjoy as much as the double claro, candella Havanas that used to be common, and my favorite commercial pipe tobacco, State Express from England, was discontinued some time ago. Cigarettes give me almost no sensual enjoyment at all. No, the reason lies far back in childhood, I'm certain of that, though it's still impossible for me to distinguish all the causative elements clearly. In part I admired my father and his "literary" ways, and he was a pipe smoker; in part I hated him and resented the alienation he forced on me and all our family. Cigarette smoking was a way to cross the immense barrier between the Carruths and the rest of the world, which I wanted to do more than anything. I wanted to be "out there" with the others, away from solitude and fear. I never made it and never will. Precisely how this dynamic knot of attraction and repulsion evolved over the years and became an ineradicable component of my being, is unknown to me. I doubt anyone could figure it out except in gross, uninteresting terms. But I know it is there, close to the heart of my psychopathological life, creative and destructive, a strength, a weakness, a function of the basic energy that has always driven me.

THE ROME THEATER in Pleasantville probably resembled small-town movie houses in the 1930s all over the country. It had been built a decade or so earlier for the showing of silent films. By 1936, the heart of the Great Depression, it was worn and shabby; it offered double features, bingo, giveaway chinaware, anything to attract audiences. Admission was fifteen cents for matinees and twenty-five in the evenings. I went as often as I could, perhaps once a week, and did not care greatly what movies were showing, with the consequence that now my memory is overladen with names, faces, and images of all kinds from the popular films of that era.

But sometimes I went furtively to a door in the back of the building. It opened off a slotlike alley. The other side of the alley was a concrete wall. Trash barrels. Broken furniture. Many shadows. When I was certain no one could see me, I slipped through the door, then up a steep, dingy stairway that brought me to another theater hidden on top of the one below. This secret theater was dark, small, filled with cigarette smoke. The seats pitched downward toward the screen at a sharp angle. The whirring of the projector could be heard distinctly, and the coruscant beam of light that shot down through the smoke to the screen was bright and straight.

Perhaps the audience numbered thirty or forty. No more than that. I remember little else about them. And what I remember of the films is only that they were different from those shown in the public theater down below: more serious. No sentimental comedies or tawdry musicals. I have the impression they were westerns, of which my parents disapproved, but also that they were about real moral and metaphysical issues, probably with a political slant. They may have been a kind of super-newsreel, news raised to the status of myth, for newsreels were often what I liked best when I went to the movies. At any rate they were not, though one might have expected it, pornographic. As I sat in the dark and watched, my feelings were fear and excitement mingled together, a sense of growing confidence which I nevertheless knew might turn out to be false. I also felt pleasantly alone. I was aware that the others scattered among the seats were experiencing similar feelings.

Maybe after all it was a kind of pornography?

Now I have a clearer if still faint remembrance of those others. They were all men. They were older than I. The projector's light reflected dimly from white shirts and here and there from bald heads and eyeglasses. They sat mostly apart from one another or in groups of two and three, and in differing attitudes – some lounging, some bent forward toward the screen.

This dream began when I was about fifteen and continued until I was in my forties.

Auden wrote somewhere that the invention of photography was the worst of the disasters of technology. I don't recall exactly what he meant. Probably he felt that photography blurred the distinction between his primary and secondary worlds, as he called them, the worlds of reality and imagination, and since this distinction was important to him, photography – the preservation of reality outside of time, which had been a function of the imagination through all earlier epochs – was troublesome. I agree that keeping this distinction in mind is important, but not that the distinction itself means much. In fact the primary and secondary worlds are interfused and we live in a fluidity of consciousness. What happens inside and outside a camera is merely a simplified analogue of what happens inside and outside a human head.

Nevertheless a filmed image, especially of a person, is a mystery. Not a puzzle; it can be rationalized easily. But it is a variable awesomeness, sometimes poignant, sometimes frightening. Only rarely is it joyful. How can that person who is dead, or who is even twenty minutes older, be there? Jung emphasized the similarity, conventionality, and recognizability of archetypal images because it suited his purpose to do so, but individuality is what makes those images powerful. A burned-out ranch may be the sack of Troy, but it is still a burned-out ranch. That man in the newsreel running and dodging down the hillside, that Spanish Republican caught at the instant when the bullet smashes his heart, that death in its individual actuality forever: this is the mystery and

awesomeness. And this, aside from the simple symbolic representation
– the womb, the initiation, the secret identity – is what my dream
was about.

WHEN I WAS TEN or eleven I had a BB gun, a standard Daisy "air rifle,"
as they were called, not air-powered, however, but spring-powered,
which I had ordered from the Sears Roebuck catalogue and paid for
with money I earned. It was the only gun I've ever owned. (Gun, from
the medieval Latin feminine name Gunilda, applied to a mangonel or
stone-throwing machine, though I don't know what to make of that – or
maybe I do.) I shot and killed two living creatures with it. One was a
medium-sized green frog by the edge of a brook; it died immediately. A
bubble formed on its back and grew larger and larger until it burst; then
a second bubble, a third, etc. The other was a chickadee on a branch of
the maple outside our attic window. I shot from well back of the window
and in the expectation that I wouldn't hit the bird, and at first I
thought I hadn't, for like the frog it didn't move. Then slowly – almost
as if thoughtfully – it tilted forward from its perch and fell to the
ground. I ran down the two flights of stairs, retrieved it, and buried it.

    Both these episodes sickened me.

    Once I also deliberately shot my younger brother Gorton point-
blank. He was wearing a heavy, stiff, horsehide jacket that had once been
mine. I was certain the impact of the BB wouldn't be felt through that
thick leather – although if I was certain why did I try it? Gorton's face
turned red and he began to cry – he was about six or seven at the time
– and I could see he wasn't putting it on; he was stung. And no doubt
shocked by my perfidy. So was I.

    I was, or became, a first-class marksman. In the army I was given a
Thompson submachine gun, which I'm glad I never had to shoot
except on the firing range. I was also given a little medal for superior
marksmanship with carbine and rifle. I had always been able to ring the
swinging bell at the shooting gallery, ten times for the ten .22 short-
shorts you could buy in those days for a quarter. Many years later when
I was fifty and my son was about ten and had his own BB gun, I picked
it up one day and shot a small twig sticking up through the snow about
twenty-five yards away. It quivered slightly when the BB struck it. The

Bo was astonished, but I wasn't. I knew I could do it. Even so I was pleased.

Yet I hate the damned things. I always will, and I hope I'll never have to shoot another gun in my life, not even a BB gun.

I remember in Woodbury an old, unused shed that stood on the ridge back of Pomperaug Road, beside the path to the river and under a hemlock tree. The wooden walls and door were weathered colorfully, all the shades of gray, silver, and brown that old softwood boards take on, with traces of ancient red paint still intermingling. One day I stood away from it and shot a pattern of copper-coated BBs into the door, and I can still see in my mind the points of new metal gleaming against the antique background, an effect that pleased me at the time. I think it still would. The particularity of it: vertical boards with knots and splits in them, square rusty nailheads, shadings of color, lichen, and then the design of the new copper BBs, a circle with a tricuspid in it. *Particular*, related to *part*, *particle*, *partisan*, *partner*, and *parse* – all pretty good words.

STEPHEN SPENDER VISITED Chicago while I was living there. I don't remember exactly when, but during the time I was active on the staff of *Poetry*, roughly between 1947 and 1950. His visit had something to do with *Poetry*, probably with raising funds, since that is what invited celebrities are invited for – what else? Most of the people connected with *Poetry* were partial to celebrities, but if they wanted one for private purposes, they were more likely to invite Governor Stevenson's ex-wife or Potter Palmer's granddaughter.

I took no part in entertaining Spender; that was the province of the poetocracy. A huge bash was organized, which I later travestied in my novel, *Appendix A*, but I remember almost nothing of it now. I was no doubt drunk. As for Spender, my impression is of a man taller by a good deal than myself, handsome, wavy hair, a good workmanlike British accent, an unpressed suit, a pleasing manner, etc. But the main point is that Spender was indeed a celebrity, one of the best-known and best-liked poets of that time in the English language. The names of Auden and Spender went together as inevitably as Laurel and Hardy. They were not only the young lions, who had baited Eliot successfully; they

were the immediate and powerful influence on the foremost young
American poets of the generation just before mine – Karl Shapiro,
Muriel Rukeyser, Randall Jarrell, Delmore Schwartz, and the other left-
leaning poets who had begun to publish just before World War II.
Auden's *Collected Poems* of 1945 and Spender's of 1942, which was
titled *Ruins and Visions*, were on the shelf of every poet and every seri-
ous reader in the country, and they were well-worn. I still recall the dust
jackets on both books. Spender seemed to me then a literary giant, as he
was, a man almost infinitely beyond my reach, and although I must have
shaken his hand and may have tried for a moment or two to hold up one
end of a conversation with him, I'm certain that my anxiety, which with
a figure as exalted as Spender could not have been much allayed by gin,
would have kept me as far away from him as I could politely get.

Many years later Spender gave a reading and talk at Syracuse Uni-
versity, and I introduced him. We chatted a little beforehand, but not
much. Our main chance to talk was at breakfast the next morning, be-
fore I took him to his plane. We ate sticky pastry and drank coffee in the
Something Room at the Hotel Syracuse downtown. In my introduction
the night before I had said that in reviewing the letters of Wyndham
Lewis I had learned that when Lewis went blind Spender was the first
person who volunteered to read to him. "I have reason to believe," I had
said, "that Mr. Spender cared no more for Lewis's rotten fascistic ideas
than I do. But in those days a community of letters existed, to which one
was admitted solely on grounds of talent and devotion, and within it a
mutual respect or even loyalty that traversed ideological disagree-
ments." Spender picked that up at breakfast. "You know," he said in that
accent I like so well, though the majority of people who speak it are
royal pains in the ass, "you hit it exactly – that business about the
community of letters. If it hadn't been for that, how could we have
stood Eliot?"

What surprised me most was Spender's appearance. Here's a man in
his eighties, I said to myself; remarkably fine-looking and vigorous, fly-
ing all around the country, giving readings and lectures almost every
day. How does he do it? And I must have hinted something of the kind,
because at one point he looked at me quizzically and a little sharply, his
coffee cup in his hand, and said: "I'm only seventy-three, you know."
Jesus! Only eleven years older than I. I was surprised; I was floored. In
Chicago he had been as far beyond me as the stars. And here we were,

two old men together, at bay, so to speak, before the immense pack of our pursuers.

Well, that's romanticizing, of course. What we were actually was something else: two elderly men eating a third-rate breakfast in a third-rate restaurant in a third-rate American city – what could be more commonplace? And we were enjoying it too, Spender as much as I. It was the kind of meeting that evokes a quick sense of kinship with someone you will almost certainly never see again and to whom you feel no obligation beyond the agreeable one of being ordinarily decent. It was a pleasure. At his reading Spender had been at pains to separate himself from Auden. At one point he even said he had not met Auden until... well, I'm not sure when, maybe 1937. But I had just read Chamberlain's biography of Auden, which contains a photograph of the two, a snapshot, taken at a time well before the date Spender mentioned. Why? Why such misremembering? At breakfast I told him how grateful I was to him for publishing some of my poems in *Encounter* at a time when I needed encouragement. "I like those poems very much," he said immediately and rapidly and with a straight face. Clearly he didn't remember them at all, any more than I remember ninety-nine percent of the poems that I have chosen as an editor over the years. No doubt the reasons for such misremembering are easy to understand in general and easy to forgive in particular; still I do my best, not always successfully, not to let them affect me.

In fact I think a good deal about these niceties of relationship between ordinary egotism and the awareness of pure subjectivity that all artists need. Spender's accomplishment on his own, as poet, critic, and editor, is creditable and good. The miserable outcome at *Encounter*, when it turned out that the magazine had been secretly financed through a front by the CIA, overtook him precisely because he is a good man. It was a classic case. He dealt with it honorably. He has no need, beyond the frivolous, to dissemble, and I hope his poems and his reputation will endure for a long time, though that's in the lap of the gods. The best and nearly only thing one can do for the gifted poets one knows is to wish them good luck, as I do.

KENNETH BURKE WAS SHORT in stature, maybe a couple of inches shorter than myself, but sturdy, straight-backed, with a good face: handsome and rugged. Gray hair and steel-rimmed glasses. He wore a rumpled gray suit, and looked the typical intellectual of the 1940s, although in many respects he wasn't typical at all. To my mind his critical writing is the most independent, honest, and useful of that period; more reasonable than Winters's, more original than Ransom's or Blackmur's, and far more mannerly and agreeable than Edmund Wilson's. His writing was awkward, granted – and difficult to follow, but it was mind-work right there on the page, pushing itself always harder, ambitious for its ends but modest in itself; none of the mock humility of Eliot or Tate. Furthermore his ideas, deriving from the socially oriented criticism of Parrington but enriched by the writerly insights of the New Critics, prefigured many of the attitudes of the poststructuralists of the past two decades, and not only prefigured them but articulated them more fully and reasonably than the younger critics recognize. As far as I know, they don't acknowledge him, or when they do they dismiss him as a mere "humanist" – that dirty word applied by every generation to the previous generation.

I met Burke only once, at a party on the south side of Chicago, I think at Harvey Webster's apartment in 1948 or 1949. I had fortified myself beforehand, as usual, but at the beginning of the party I was still very tense. I found myself on a sofa beside Burke. He chatted, I listened. I tried to act as if I were comfortable, as I supposed the editor of *Poetry* should be, while the party began warming up and getting noisier. People standing in clusters, looming above us, talking loudly, etc. Burke leaned toward me and said: "I wrote a poem this afternoon. Would you like to hear it?" I said: "Of course." (What else?) He recited it in a low voice directly into my ear, and I didn't catch a word – not one. But because the poem was brief, because the occasion was social and cheery, I assumed the poem was funny, some sort of epigram, and I laughed. Immediately Burke drew back. He looked at me with shock, indignation, and injury.

I had blundered. I saw in him instantly the soul of the devotee, as I had seen it so often in all kinds of people. Burke took his poems seriously, even if no one else did. And in truth they weren't great, I think, though I haven't looked at them for many years.

I accused myself bitterly. What stupidity! Here was a person I would have liked to know, to be friendly with – if circumstances permitted – someone I admired genuinely, i.e., for his work. It was more than that; it was the mind revealed in the work, the intellectual exuberance, which for me remains the most attractive quality of that era. How I miss it now, surrounded as I am – we are – by apathy and mediocrity. But my timorousness, unrelenting from infancy until this moment, had caused me to offend Burke, so that again I had lost the chance I wanted to know my own kind; and because I was so good an actor, like most anxious people, and could disguise my fear in suavity – though not real suavity, just the alcoholic kind – Burke did not conceive why I had done it. Laughter in the face of a beautiful poem. It was unaccountable. I remember nothing more from that party. No doubt I either got drunk or left early and then got drunk. That was how it was.

IT SEEMS TO ME I can remember the look of each bookcase in the Woodbury house, and in the Pleasantville house too, and the exact location of every title. I saw them often enough. But of course I can't really remember them that well, and in my mind now, fifty years later, I see only fragments through a mist, the lower dark corner of the bookcase at the top of the stairs, the second shelf of the one with the glass front in the living room. They held dingy old books mostly, which my father had bought for nickels and dimes from the Salvation Army in Waterbury, part of his relentless self-education. *The Poetical Works of A. Pope, Mr. Britling Sees It Through, Adventures in the Andes, Memoirs of a Revolutionist, The Cricket on the Hearth, The Old Wives' Tale, History of the Conquest of Peru* (3 vols.), *History of the Netherlands* (6 vols.), etc.

I looked into these books often and read what I liked here and there. Sometimes a book like Bulfinch's *Mythology* would hold me spellbound and call me back again and again, in which case I was always a little surprised, because the general air of dilapidation about those books somewhat repelled and frightened me. A few books were so utterly fusty that I never touched them.

I remember one book on the bottom shelf of that bookcase at the top of the stairs. You couldn't miss it: there it was, dead ahead, as your eyes rose above floor level when you were climbing up. I saw it thousands of times. The title on the spine was:

NERVOUS

NESS

Another ghastly morality novel, I thought to myself every time, about some ghastly forlorn girl of the moors named Ness. And hadn't I already at age thirteen read all of Scott, Cooper, Irving, Dickens, Stevenson, and even some of Hardy? – and had enjoyed them too, though sometimes the enjoyment was an effort, a kind of dutiful effort. Enough, I said. I would read *Tarzan of the Apes* and the novels of Zane Grey in the public library on Wednesday and Friday afternoons, sitting under the big round table. I smell the dust and oil of the old wooden floor to this day. Never did I dare bring such books home, however; they weren't explicitly forbidden, but I knew they were "trashy" and "not the right reading matter for an intelligent child," as my father would have said. Once when I told him I had read a book of poems by Robert W. Service and had memorized a couple of them, he looked at me with patient condescension and said – but of course I don't remember the words. I remember the look. The purport of his words was clear enough.

Years later when I was in my thirties and was again living at home with my parents, I pulled that book from the shelf at the top of the stairs and sat on the step to look at it, still thinking, since I am literal-minded and not quick-witted, that it was a novel entitled *Nervous Ness*. I saw at once, of course, that it was a book of pre-Freudian practical psychology; the hyphen which had originally divided the title had been worn off. How many hands had held that book? I had no idea, but I was touched by the thought. I was myself ill at that time, unable to exist in the world, and I was thinking a good deal about my parents, especially my father, and my relationship with them. My father was ill too – I think I had known it intuitively since childhood – but he had hidden it all his life, and had found ways to live around his phobias, to exist on the edges of them. But he had not hidden his illness from himself. He had bought this old book and probably had read it, trying to understand. I thumbed the pages, testing passages at random, passages that seemed to me both ludicrous in their concepts and urgent in their sincerity. Had the book helped my father? I couldn't see how. But who knows what will help another person who is desperate enough?

I remember another time ten years earlier, when I had been in psychoanalysis in Chicago for a couple of years. I was on a holiday visit with my parents. At the dinner table I referred to myself, I don't recall in what connection, as "neurotic," which was how all young people referred to themselves in those days; the word was commonplace. At once loudly and indignantly my father said: "You're not neurotic!" I shut up. I could see how deeply shocked he was. For him, like many of his generation, neurosis was equivalent to madness. His shock lasted a long time, and although later on, when I was hospitalized and then for a considerable period lived in total seclusion, he grew used to the idea of a neurotic son, I think he never overcame the feeling that I was therefore crazy and dangerous. One time when he visited me in the hospital, I became angry enough over my continued confinement to show it, which was rare for me. I punched a wardrobe and splintered the door-panel. My father ran from the room. He accosted the first attendant he found. "The boy's in bad shape," I heard him say, his voice shaking. Well, it's true, I was in bad shape, but not the way my father meant it. Punching that door – in effect punching my father, which I could never, never have done – was a very sane thing to do at that moment and in those circumstances. None of the hospital staff complained about it at all.

I wonder if my father ever punched a door.

Books. Lots of books. My childhood was surrounded with them. They reposed there on the shelves in their umbrageous hundreds. I believe I thought, when I was a young child, that they were alive, or had been alive, or were ghostly presences talking among themselves behind my back. At any rate I knew they were important, fusty or not, and in some way menacing. That knowledge has shaped my life.

ONE TIME IN THE LATE sixties I had to obtain some arsenic. It had been prescribed by a doctor for my wife, Rose Marie, and it had to be in a suspension. I went out on a Saturday morning to the local druggist, but he couldn't do it. He would need to order the medicine, he said, and it would take some days to get it. I went to a pharmacy in a nearby larger town. The druggist there said the same thing. "A suspension is not an emulsion or a solution," he added, by way of condescending professional mystification. "I know," I said. "I worked in a drugstore when I was a kid. And in those days a self-respecting pharmacist could compound a suspension right there in his shop." He was not fazed, nor was any other druggist in northern Vermont, from Burlington to St. Johnsbury, from Montpelier to Newport. In half a day or more I drove my pickup over the whole region. But I failed.

When I reached home, a strange car with Connecticut plates was in front of the house. I was not greatly in need of visitors at that point, but I went into the kitchen quickly, and there at the old and scarred round oak table was Mark Van Doren. I recognized him at once from his photos on book jackets. The woman next to him, I knew, must be Dorothy, his wife. Rose Marie, who was sitting with them and had served coffee and kuchen, began to introduce us, but already Mark and I had shaken hands warmly. And then, after I had poured myself some coffee at the stove and we all had sat down again, I learned how extra-ordinarily kind some older writers can be. Mark recited to me by heart a quite long passage from the second section of my poem called *Journey to a Known Place*.

At that time – as earlier and later – I scarcely thought of myself as a poet at all. I was living mostly in seclusion, though beginning to get around more than I had during the previous fifteen years. My work was largely, say ninety-five percent, unconnected with my poetry, and much of it was outdoors in the company of people who considered me a laborer or mechanic, never a writer – at least it was never openly ac-knowledged among us. For long periods I forgot I was a poet. I needed visits (usually in summer) with my few friends who were writers, like Denise Levertov and Adrienne Rich, to remind me of my real function, to revalidate me. When *Journey* had first been published in 1961, I had been living in Norfolk, Connecticut, only a few miles from Mark's home in Falls Village. At the suggestion of James Laughlin, my publisher and friend, I had sent Mark a copy of the book, and had received a cordial and generous letter in response; I had said to myself that I should call on him, I had even driven a number of times past the house I thought was his – I never found out if it was – and tried to hype myself into stopping; but I was too shy, I couldn't do it. Then seven or eight years later he and Dorothy were there in my own kitchen, two hundred miles north of Connecticut, at my own table. I don't know if other people can understand the quality of that experience for me. It was astonishment, almost incredulity. It was the gift of unexpected faith, the opening of the heavens. I choose these words with care, for although I have no con-ventional religious belief, I think I know what those have felt who have witnessed miracles.

Mark liked my poetry. The visit, the reciting of my lines, could mean nothing else. And I always liked his. The work of people like Van Doren has always moved me in a special way, people talented, intelligent, devoted, and humane – Archibald MacLeish was another – who have written superb, unimprovable poems, but whose work does not place them in the first rank and is perhaps in danger of being forgotten. Because the place of such poets in our consciousness is fragile, I hold them dearer than the titans, who can take care of themselves, and do. Mark was not a great poet, as the term is commonly understood, but he wrote some great poems. And he was a great teacher, a great human being. Many others who knew him better than I, especially those who were his students at Columbia, as diverse as Thomas Merton, John Berryman, and Allen Ginsberg, have said the same thing.

After that visit Mark and I wrote brief letters back and forth, nothing high-powered or literary, just little notes of encouragement, bits about birds and trees – that sort of thing. Then Mark died. I exchanged a few notes with Dorothy, and then she died too. I felt the awful steadiness of the turning wheel – poets working, aging, dying, being replaced – the inexorability of it. And the pathos. These were nothing new in my life, of course. But perhaps it was then, when I was in my late forties, that they began to enlarge themselves in my awareness exceedingly, as they have ever since.

As for the arsenic, our local druggist ordered it and eventually we got it.

ONCE IN A POEM I called it the "blue house in the guttering chestnut forest." In fact it was painted gray with a bluish tint, and although some American chestnut trees still survived when I was a boy, we had no forest, at least not nearby. The house was a farmhouse originally, plain and simple, built early in the eighteenth century, sided with clapboards. The roof was a modified saltbox. It had wide pine floorboards inside, an enclosed staircase, small-paned windows; some of the glass was original, and had wavy, rainbow-colored patterns in it, with the maker's initials scratched in a corner. The immediate surroundings – my father owned four acres – still resembled a farmyard: the "north field," a grassy expanse with a knoll and a hollow, the "orchard" on the southeast, a plantation of eight or ten apple trees. The house was on a little hill, thirty feet above the road, and the front yard sloped downward to a steep bank. It had two immense sugar maples, whose roots ran along the surface and whose foliage shaded out the "lawn," which was no more than wispy tufts of grass.

Beyond our property lay other fields, growing up to sumac, willow, birch, and locust. I don't know who owned them.

The original barn, across the road, was owned by a family named Fray, who had a somewhat more modern house, probably from about 1900, next to the barn. Ralph Fray, a year younger than I, was my closest friend. He was a strong, stocky boy, more than my match at wrestling, and a good-looking boy as well, with dark hair and brown eyes. The Frays believed they had Indian blood in them, as most rural New Englanders of that time did, and in spite of the fact that the idea of the "noble savage," having filtered down through who knows how many layers of romantic consciousness, was widely popular at that time, I see no reason to doubt that this was so.

My own people came, on my father's side, from Scotch-Irish stock, two brothers, John and William Carruth, who were refugees from King James's Ulster Plantation – to which they had been forcibly removed from Dumfries and where they had learned to starve as well in Ireland as they had in Scotland. They settled in Massachusetts in 1710. Other Carruths emigrated later to other parts of North America. The family here is larger than one might expect; many times I have found Carruths in local phone books all over the country. My own branch has no Indian blood, as far as I know, but over the generations it has absorbed plenty of English, Dutch, French, Scandinavian, etc. I don't know what real value resides in the notion of "nativeness," probably not much, but for what it's worth the Carruths, like the Frays and millions of others, are native Americans, if only because they can't be anything else.

Our house was supported by its chimney, the same principle of engineering used in many skyscrapers, the frame suspended from a central stem or core. My memory probably is distorted, but when I envision the cellar of that house, I see a chimney ten-feet square or more, occupying much of the space. It was made of rough stone and mortar, and the great hand-hewn beams, with the marks of the broadaxe on them, perhaps twelve-by-twelve-inches thick, passed through the chimney walls in both directions, north-south and east-west. I think those four great timbers carried the whole weight of the house. The outer walls of the cellar were made from field stone without mortar, and they bulged inward. They were firm enough, I suppose, they kept the earth from falling into the cellar, but clearly they did not support much weight, and it was easy to be a little frightened when you looked at them. That huge chimney tapered as it ascended through the first and second stories, then in the attic became an ordinary brick chimney. For several years I slept next to it up there, sharing the attic with a colony of bats. At night the bats sailed back and forth over my head; by day they clung to the inside of the unplastered splitlath of the north gable. Red squirrels came in sometimes too, and in the big maple outside the window orioles nested in summer and tanagers flittered. I liked all these creatures. Indeed, I liked all wild animals, and some of my favorite books were by John Burroughs and Ernest Thompson Seton. Once when my father picked a green snake (*Liopeltis vernalis*) out of a lilac bush and was bitten on the thumb, I thought he got what he deserved.

When I was a soldier in Italy, the lizards there crept and ran all over our tents and mosquito bars. It was common to awaken in the morning and see, first thing, a lizard fifteen inches away, peering into one's eyes. Outdoors the lizards, which looked like miniature dinosaurs with ridged spines and bulky shoulders, played fighting games in the grass, often close to my feet when I sat under an olive tree, fierce games, though I never saw any injury beyond the loss of the detachable tails. If I lay down with my eyes at grass level and watched the lizards, I could see the rampaging dinosaurs and great ferns of the Mesozoic era. In the American west, the Rockies and Sierras, I have myself played games, mostly strife-of-the-eyes or who-can be-dead-the-longest, with rattlesnakes. The snakes always won. Once near Buck-Eye Flat in the Sequoia National Forest I came suddenly on a massasauga stretched out and sunning itself on a bank by the side of a path. I stood still. We looked at each other, green eye vs. black eye, for as long as I could stand it, maybe fifteen minutes, and during much of that time a newly hatched white lacewing walked waveringly up and down the length of the snake's back. The snake didn't move a muscle, didn't twitch; seeing it made my own back itch. Finally I turned my head aside for an instant, and then the snake was gone.

When I was younger, I had a small bedroom on the second floor, with one window. The floor of wide pine boards, what they used to call pumpkin pine, was humped and wrenched, almost convulsively. A couple of the boards were warped upward a good four inches above the general level. My father was a fine carpenter, and he had restored much of the first floor of the house, but did not get to the second before we had to move away. He had truly astonishing patience; I never saw him express the slightest irritation when things went wrong. My own experience, though I have worked a good deal with hand tools, is just the opposite. Nothing infuriates me more quickly than a rusted bolt that snaps its head off under the pressure of my wrench, or a board mismeasured, an eighth of an inch too short for the space it's intended to fill. I have the impression that my father never misjudged a bolt or mismeasured anything, and that all his boards were sawn exactly right.

In that small bedroom on the second floor I used to wake at five o'clock A.M. or earlier, often I think at three-thirty or four o'clock (insomnia has been with me lifelong), and I would lie in bed and read until the rest of the family got up. My father had taught me to read when I was four. He used an old primer, which he probably bought for a nickel at the Salvation Army in Waterbury, and the lessons were a half hour every morning before breakfast. I learned quickly, and in my boyhood I read many, many books, for which I'm thankful now. But in those years it seemed to me that my father's instruction had merely placed me ahead of my class in school, and for a while – until I learned to play dumb – I was segregated from the others on that account.

WHEN MY WIFE AND I and our infant son moved to northern Vermont and settled in a location that seemed at that time remote – and in fact it was – we did so because we had to. We'd have preferred to live farther south, near our friends and relatives. But we had little money and little income, and our search for a place we could afford, which would also be immediately habitable, was unsuccessful in Connecticut, Massachusetts, and southern and central Vermont. We kept heading north, calling real estate agents who were listed in a guide published by the Vermont Development Council. After we crossed an imaginary line from Burlington to Montpelier to St. Johnsbury, real estate values declined remarkably. The north was at that time poor country, shabby, a region of marginal farms and small towns that looked worn out. Three miles into the hills from one such town, on a dirt road by the side of a brook, we found a five-room house and eleven acres of land, which we bought for $5,800.

We hoped we could afford it. We paid $3,000 down – all we had – and took a fifteen-year mortgage for the rest. Our monthly payment to the bank would be $27.54, and we thought we could manage that. We felt lucky and greatly relieved to have found a place where we hoped to live on our meager resources. For a while this had seemed impossible. Indeed it would have been impossible a few years later. When we settled in northern Vermont, land was selling for $25 an acre, but not long after we arrived an influx of well-to-do people began and land values were inflated by 1,000 percent in less than a decade. Extreme northern New England was the only part of the northeast that hadn't already been exploited in 1960. If I'd been smart – but I never am – I'd have borrowed a little more money from the bank and bought a thousand acres. And today I'd be a yuppie.

Our new home was adequate, but no more. The house had no central heating, but instead a kerosene pot-burner in the living room and a wood-burning range in the kitchen; in winter we kept warm, though the two rooms upstairs couldn't be used for anything but sleeping. The water supply was a siphon-fed line from a spring located on a neighbor's place some distance down the road. The kitchen had one tap that gave a thin flow of water into a cast-iron sink. We did our laundry, including the child's diapers, in the brook, which was icy cold. About thirty yards from the house was a cowshed, in effect a one-cow barn, nine-by-nine feet, with a stall and stanchion and a hole in the wall, covered by a leather-hinged flap, through which to throw the manure. I put in a window, took out the stall and stanchion, laid a new floor, boarded up the interior walls, installed a small box-stove from the junk store, and the cowshed became my workplace for the next twenty years, giving us what amounted to an extra room. On wet days it always smelled of cow. At first I worked by lanternlight after dark, but then I ran a line from the house and gave myself electricity. It was a dusty, sooty, shabby, and extremely cramped place to work, but before long I became attached to it, and I still think of it fondly. Then before the first winter came I put a cattle trough in the cellar of the house to hold water, fixed up a pump and pressure tank, and bought a secondhand hot-water heater, so that we could have a washing machine and take baths without heating water on the stove.

Over the years we made other improvements. I rebuilt the kitchen, and put in a new sink and new plumbing, though we always used the

woodstove for cooking and heating. I hired a local person to install a
new bathroom and a modern septic system. I built bookshelves. We re-
painted the woodwork and repapered the walls. All this took a long
time, many years, because we were so busy with the daily routine that
we could seldom take time for anything extra. And we continued to live
poor, as country people say. We bought our appliances secondhand and
our clothing from the church rummage sales. I learned to make all my
own repairs; I became a country mechanic, plumber, electrician, and
carpenter. After a while I even learned to sweat a copper fitting as neatly
as a professional. I learned to repair my cars, even to the extent of com-
plete engine overhauls. I cut, split, transported, and stacked ten cords of
firewood each summer to run the stoves in the kitchen and cowshed
during the winter; this took thirty days a year. I did evening barn chores
with a neighboring farmer in return for milk, and I mended fence, made
hay, cultivated potatoes, and did nearly every other kind of farmwork. I
built a woodshed, a chicken coop, a duck house. I made a big garden,
160-by-200 feet, in which we raised enough potatoes, corn, squash,
green vegetables, root vegetables, etc., to feed us for a year; at first we
canned them, but later we bought a secondhand freezer and froze them.
We picked wild berries and ate fiddleheads and lamb's quarters. We
kept a small flock of hens for eggs and meat, also ducks and geese, and
we occasionally went in with friends to raise a pig or a cow, or we bought
them cheaply from neighboring farmers. The one thing I did not do
that poor country people usually rely on – and this may have been a
mistake – was to hunt and fish. I had no liking for blood sports. But we
gratefully accepted venison, rabbit, trout, and perch from friends and
neighbors.

     All my life I have been a compulsive worker, but I've never worked as
hard at any other time as I did during this period in Vermont. Usually
I worked in the woods and fields or in the garden, or did errands and re-
pairs and house chores, during the daytime, especially in summer when
the big garden always needed attention, and then worked in the cow-
shed at night. I wrote book reviews for newspapers and literary maga-
zines, I read and copyedited manuscripts and wrote ad copy for book
publishers, I did rewriting and ghostwriting – at one time I had more
books on the market with other people's names on the title pages than
books of my own. I did anything I could and accepted every assignment
that came to me, always afraid that if I turned one down the editors

would cross me off their list. Once I was the sole staff of the monthly newsletter of an occult book club on Long Island. But I was no good at selling myself, and could not go down to New York to seek jobs from the editors and publishers there; I had to do everything by mail. Nor could I turn out the kind of material that would be acceptable to high-paying magazines. I tried, I even had an agent who urged me to give him things to sell to *Holiday*, *Harper's Bazaar*, etc., and who suggested topics and approaches, but it just wasn't in me; after a while I quit trying. Consequently my income from my editorial hackwork was low. In the 1960s I averaged $3,000 or $4,000 a year before taxes, gradually rising to around $10,000 in the later 1970s when I was doing regular stints for the *Chicago Daily News*, *Bookletter*, and *Harper's*. In some of the bad years we had emergency grants of $500 from PEN or the Author's League, which helped immensely; I never knew who was responsible for them, but to this day I'm grateful. And other grants, fellowships, and prizes were helpful too. But by 1979, I was worn out, and my son was at the university. The System had snagged me after all. I needed more cash than I could earn, even though by that time I was spending eighty or ninety hours a week in the cowshed during the winters. Always before, when I'd been asked to teach at universities around the country, I had declined, because I knew I couldn't face a class of students, but in the fall of 1979, apprehensively, I went to work at Syracuse University. The semimonthly paycheck was a blessing I knew nothing about teaching, of course, but my editorial and literary doctoring skills were useful in the creative writing program, and gradually I became comfortable in my new profession.

The truth, as readers of my work know, is that I've suffered all my life from chronic psychiatric disorders that were acute during my thirties and have been slowly and painfully – and imperfectly – overcome in the years since then. The decade before I moved to Vermont was spent in almost complete invalidism, including a long spell of hospitalization and a longer spell of reclusion. When I remarried at the age of forty, I was well enough to shift from reclusion to seclusion, but I still could not do what literary people normally do with their lives – work in offices or class-rooms, live in a city, use public transportation, go to theaters, literary parties, etc. So I couldn't earn much money and I needed a quiet and private place to live. That's why I found myself in the backcountry of northern Vermont with a young wife – who was a refugee from eastern

Europe and had been cheated of her education by the war; during the following years she obtained a high school equivalency diploma and bachelor's and master's degrees – and an infant son. When our friends in the counterculture of the 1960s, many of whom had come from Bethesda or Greenwich and had nice little independent incomes, praised my wife and me for living in "voluntary poverty," we laughed.

When did I write my poetry? Usually at the tag end of the night, three or four o'clock. Occasionally I could steal a day for myself. But always I had to be sure that everything else was squared away – deadlines, chores, errands, fieldwork, maintenance, reviews, hack editing – before I could turn to my own writing; that was part of my compulsiveness. Or was it simple necessity? When the roof leaks you'd better fix it. When your wife needs something you'd better get it for her. I learned to write fast and revise with lightning speed, like a newspaper deskman, which at one time and briefly I had been. I admire and envy my friends, people like John Haines and Galway Kinnell, who can spend months or years on a poem and can put their own work ahead of everything else. I can't do it, and perhaps this, as much as matters of principle, is what has influenced me to believe that artists should not be given any more consideration than other people: there's nothing sacred, or even all that special, about a poem. Though I owe much to Ezra Pound, I rebel against his idea of the poet as philosopher king, which seems to me both dangerous and a concomitant, if not a cause, of his foolish politics. Once in 1965 I was able to give myself a whole month. I don't remember how this came about, but I wrote "Contra Mortem," a poem in thirty parts, during that month, doing one part a day for thirty days. (Later I found the wonderful epigraph from Lao-tzu, which fits so well.) This poem remains my personal favorite among all the poems I've written, though not many share my feeling. Later in the seventies and eighties I was granted a number of residencies at Yaddo, the artists' retreat at Saratoga Springs, where I could put everything else out of my mind. Much of *The Sleeping Beauty* was written there, and many other poems and essays as well.

But voluntary or not, the life of poverty we lived in Vermont is what we would have chosen anyway six months after we settled there. This is what is important. It was a hard life and we could have benefited from more leisure and less financial anxiety – which were factors in the eventual separation of my wife and me – but it was in the fullest sense a rewarding life. And it was a possible life, nothing like poverty in the ghetto or in some ruined part of the world. Winters in northern Vermont are long, cold, and snowy, but we stayed warm in our banked and caulked little dwelling even when it was thirty or forty below outside, snug in our bed with all our clothes on and heated stones for our feet; I learned to love the winter, the cleanness and clarity of it, in spite of frostbite from the bitter wind and backache from shoveling snow. And this kind of adaptation occurred in every aspect of life there. What those years and that place afforded me was an opportunity to put everything together, the land and seasons, the people, my family, my work, my evolving sense of survival (for when I'd been in the hospital the doctors had told me I'd never again have anything like a normal life), in one tightly integrated imaginative structure. The results were my poems, for what they're worth, and in my life a very gradual but perceptible triumph over the internal snarls and screw-ups that had crippled me from childhood on. How gratifying it was! The process had begun before I went to Vermont, of course, with changes in my perception of myself and the world that turned me inside out and upside down, and it has continued since I was forced to leave (forced because no one in Vermont would hire me), but the time there was crucial. And I'm not sure I could have done the same thing to the same degree anywhere else.

In 1974, I think, I was awarded the Governor's Medal for Excellence in the Arts. Only one a year is given. No money is attached to it. But the ceremony in the governor's office in Montpelier was the first public occasion I had taken part in for twenty-five years, and that meant a great deal to me. Then having the recognition of my adopted state meant a great deal too. I still like that medal better than any other prize I've won. In 1978 at the age of fifty-seven I gave my first poetry reading, helped and supported by friends, in a small art gallery above a savings bank in the town of Chelsea. It was a big occasion, all the more since what had precipitated me into psychotherapy the first time, when I was twenty-five, was a poetry reading in Chicago that I ran away from. Then in 1982 I gave a reading at the Library of Congress before a quite large audience. It was a fantastic private victory. I wanted to tell someone about it, but no one was left in my life who had known me well when I was twenty-five. In the hotel I wrote a little note to my first wife, who was probably astonished to get it.

A life of hardship that was nevertheless possible was the luckiest thing that could have happened to me in my middle age. If I didn't choose it, I quickly acquiesced in it. And in a way I did choose it because the instincts that were pushing me had pushed me in that direction. My grandfather, whom I admired greatly and after whom I was named, had established himself in the Dakota Territory in 1885, and had lived there and written poems and stories there, in spite of similar hardship. I don't think I was consciously following his example and in fact his life and mine have been distinctly different, but that strain of Carruthian stubbornness and adventuresomeness was somewhere in me, buried and hard to find. In the end it saw me through – with lots of help from others along the way.

The young people I encounter today, mostly graduate students in the creative writing program at Syracuse, have nothing like this in their lives. In general they are too young to have it. But what worries me is that they don't recognize its value, they are aimed in the opposite direction, not toward the difficult but toward the easy. Everything in their upbringings and educations has trained them to seek the easy way, which is now the American way. Our lives are supposed to be "fun" and not much else. And for my young students the easy way is teaching; as quickly as they can they want to get their degrees and find niches in the academic world that will give them semimonthly paychecks in return for the least possible effort and discomfort. My friends, don't do it. Not when you're young, not even when you're middle-aged. It isn't because there's something intrinsically wrong with academic life, though I think now, as opposed to forty-five years ago when I was a grad student at the University of Chicago, that this may be the case, but because it's too easy. You believe your writing can be a separate part of your life, but it can't. A writer's writing occurs in the midst of, and by means of, all the materials of life, not just a selected few. And if your life is easy, your writing will be slack and purposeless. I'm generalizing, of course; but my main drift is sound and important. You need difficulty, you need necessity. And it isn't a paradox that you can choose necessity, can actually create necessity, if you seek the right objectives; not the great metaphysical necessity, but your own personal necessity; and it will be no less inexorable because you have chosen it. Once you are in it, your writing will be in it too.

Think of what Tom McGrath and Toni Morrison and Patrick Kavanagh and Cesare Pavese and Robert Frost have done with rural poverty. Compare their work to poems and stories about life in the academy. The latter are nearly all weak and foolish. Why? Because life in the academy is too easy. The authors of poems and stories about it do not react from it or against it, they accept it, they go with it – they are conformable; whereas good writing, from Alexander Pope to Emily Dickinson, is almost always against something. The young academicians take the basic structure and values of the academy for granted, even when they think they don't.

Yet has not the corporate structure of education done us as much harm as the corporate structures of manufacturing, selling, and thought control?

Myself, I think the aspect of necessity that helps the most is physical, and I don't mean jogging or tennis. Country people, primitive people everywhere, are healthy because their lives force them to be healthy. I don't mean they always eat the right foods or refrain from smoking, drinking, etc. I suppose most of them also take the easy, comfortable way if they can. But artists who choose necessity do so in an act of intelligence, and intelligence will still be with them after their choice. Hard necessary physical work is the best aid to composition I know.

Maybe on the other hand the best part of necessity is loving. Young people who tell me they will never marry, never have children, worry me even more than those who say they want to teach. My son David, whom I call the Bo, was central to everything I did during those years in Vermont. He was growing as I was regrowing. Because his mother was often working or going to school, but also because I wanted it, we spent a lot of time together. My love for him and his for me infused all my work. I can't imagine that work without him – or his mother too. We were a loving family. I know many great artists have worked without this element in their lives, e.g., Van Gogh, Emily Dickinson; this was their hardship. But obviously they'd have been better off personally if they'd had it, and I'm not convinced that if they had had it, their work wouldn't be just as good as it is. For me, loving and being loved were necessities. My responsibilities to others did not make me feel less responsible to my work, as young people fear. On the contrary, the point of my life was to combine the responsibilities, to make them go together in one passage, one congeries of enactments, one passion, in spite of the stresses induced by lack of time and money. This was possible. It was done. Naturally it didn't last forever.

Well, there are many kinds of necessity. A discussion of the possibilities in particular lives would be useless. But I believe nothing worth much ever came out of easy necessity, and I believe this is true on all levels and in all spheres. It is something for young artists to bear in mind. Voluntary poverty is not such a bad idea.

Suicide

To BE FRANK – and in the present case anything else would defeat the purpose, which is not poetic – no topic in fifty years of writing has blocked me as thoroughly and persistently as this one, my own suicide. For six months and more I have been unable to write anything that pleases me. Why not skip it then and go on to something else? One needn't and can't turn every event into a piece of writing. Sometimes in the past I've made this skipping maneuver and dropped a whole aspect of my life out of my literary consciousness, and then have been able in a short while to go on to other things. But that won't work now, and the reason why it won't is what I want to elucidate if I can, hoping to free myself and so return to the normal life, if there is such a thing, of a writer.

But this may not work either, because I do not wish to make public the circumstances, including peripheral actors, in which the suicide occurred; they are private and should remain private. Yet these circumstances may be precisely the factors that are causing my blockage, and what do I do then – give up being a writer? This would mean casting away the whole mental and emotional apparatus I have acquired, by luck and hard study, in a lifetime devoted to many kinds of writing. I'm sixty-seven years old. Obviously I'd be reluctant to take such a course. But I know I may have to, and if it comes to that I'm not altogether unwilling.

Early in the morning of February 24, 1988, I intentionally and massively overdosed myself with every pill I possessed. Since I had been treated by doctors over many years for insomnia, anxiety, depression, cardiac irregularity, occasional spinal pain, and I don't remember what else – except that I'm by nature hypochondriacal and usually go to the doctor three or four times a year no matter what – and moreover since no one in the past, meaning primarily my doctors, had ever suspected me of suicidal propensities, I had a fair collection of partly used bottles of medication. I opened them one after another and washed the contents down with loathsome port wine which someone had sent me from California. I was surprised, not disagreeably, by the quickness of the effect. It seems to me still that I began to feel myself going under immediately and that the process itself lasted no more than a few seconds – though I know from what I was told afterward that this cannot be true – just long enough for me to experience a sense of relief amounting to euphoria and to tell myself that this was the first time I'd been happy in years. The next thing I knew I was flat on my back, too weak to stir, with nurses, doctors, relatives, and friends staring down at me. Again I was surprised, and again not disagreeably. In fact I was astounded. How could this be? I thought to myself, this guy is invincible, he's like the soldier in battle who believes he can't be killed and consequently isn't, he's never going to die. Then right away: that's a myth, that's poetry. Even in the turbulence of awakening, my mind was literary.

I was in the intensive care unit of a hospital, of course, which is anything but poetic. I awoke fourteen or fifteen hours, I think, after I had lost consciousness, though to this day I have no clear notion of the sequence of events or the length of time they took. In fact for several months after I was discharged from the hospital I thought the whole episode had occurred a week later than it did, and I learned my error only when the bill from the hospital, giving the date of my admittance, finally reached me after its useless meandering in Medicare. For a while after I awoke – maybe a day, maybe longer – I drifted in and out of consciousness. I remember somebody saying, "This guy isn't going to make it." I remember a nurse saying, "Hayden, we have to give you a shot now, we have to paralyze you," followed by a dream-vision in which I saw my own body as a heap of jumbled bricks that all at once sprang into neatly ordered rigidity, a wall – not in the least painful. But I was indeed paralyzed, couldn't move a muscle. Afterward I was told this had been necessary because I was pulling the tubes from my mouth and nose with my hands. I remember bright lights and electronic noises. I remember someone remarking, "He can't weigh that much, he's got a potbelly but it's not as big as mine." I remember occasional sharp pains in my stomach or my hands and arms, pains that subsided almost instantly. Etc. But now I cannot put these sensations and scraps of language into any consecutive order.

Gradually but, everything considered, quite rapidly, I returned to full consciousness. I found myself with tubes in my mouth and nose, one of which passed between my vocal cords and prevented me from making a sound, IVs in my arms and hands, an arterial tap in one wrist, catheters in my heart and bladder, a respirator that wheezed rhythmically somewhere out of my line of vision and was apparently in control of my breathing, and numerous electronic monitoring devices attached to me here and there. I was not uncomfortable. Presumably I was being drenched with painkillers. I dozed a good deal. Once or twice I made panicky attempts to communicate, first by trying to speak or at least whisper or at least make intelligible mouth movements, all to no avail, and then by trying to write with a pencil and pad that were put in my hands; but I was unable to form a legible word. I had to give up and content myself with nods and smiles, which most of the time was easy. After a while, perhaps a couple of days, some of the tubes were removed, and an oxygen mask (wet and ill-smelling) was attached to my face. After several more days the mask was replaced with a double tube running on either side of my head and ending in two little nozzles fitted into my nose. I came to despise the odor of oxygen, though I was told it has no odor, and then to understand that it was all in my head, that actually I had no remaining sense of taste or smell at all. They were gone. Would they come back? The nurses said probably. The food brought to me on trays tasted and smelled like oxygen or what I took to be oxygen, a chemical smell that could more accurately have been formaldehyde. Months later, I still smell it occasionally; it seems to exude from my fingers. I had no appetite, no taste for anything but ginger ale, though I tried to force something down at each mealtime. I was x-rayed several times a day and my blood was constantly tested for its content of gases – mostly oxygen, I presume. Finally, days later, the oxygen was turned off momentarily and I was permitted to disengage from the cardiac monitors long enough to go to the bathroom. I could sit in a chair from time to time. I was even taken for a wobbly stroll around the center of the ICU with a nurse holding me by the arm.

Twice I sneaked a cigarette from the pack I'd had in my dressing gown, along with matches, before I came to the hospital. Apparently no one had bothered to look in the pockets. I blew the smoke toward the ventilator, and never knew whether anyone detected the smell or not. The fact that I was using fire only a couple of feet from the apparatus controlling the oxygen and that this was dangerous, to say the least, did not occur to me. Then once late at night a nurse, a very likable, kind-hearted nurse who was a smoker, took me to the nurses' lounge, where we each smoked a cigarette. It made me cough, and later I found out that that cough had been recorded on my dossier as a bad sign. Otherwise I went without tobacco, and I suffered from this a good deal.

As I say, however, the physical pain was not bad. What I had ex-
pected to hurt me, such as the removal of catheters, really didn't, though
when they pulled the catheter out of my heart I had a brief unpleasant
sensation of being turned inside out. The worst was that the doctors
would prescribe no aid for sleeping. When I asked my principal doctor
for a sleeping pill, he spun on one foot and motioned outward with both
hands, like an umpire signifying a foul ball: "I'll be damned if I'll give
you a sleeping pill," and he stomped out. In the circumstances I couldn't
blame him exactly, but I did wonder if he'd had any experience, per-
sonal or professional, with chronic insomnia. After I had recovered
enough strength to stay awake, I think on the third night, I lay for five
days and nights without a wink, 120 hours, which is a record for me.
At one point I wrote a half-delirious "poem" in my head about sleep
deprivation as a means of torture. I even wrote down parts of it I could
remember the next morning. As poetry it was disjointed and sloppy. But
it described accurately enough how I felt: weak, jittery, more than a little
crazy. At night in the light of a small lamp that was part of the monitor-
ing console I read crime fiction, books that people bought for me at the
drugstore, and sometimes I played extended jam sessions in my head,
hours and hours of blues, up-tempo, moderate, or draggy. At other
times I felt enraptured for no reason I could ascertain. I watched the
heart monitor on the console behind my right shoulder until my neck
got sore from being twisted. That little green puppy leapt endlessly for
the unreachable biscuit, each time falling back and springing up again.
I experimented with controlling my pulse rate and discovered I could
bring it down to about 75 by consciously relaxing myself, though most
of the time it remained at 90 or higher. As their shifts changed, by day,
evening, and night, I talked with the nurses when they were between
chores, sweet-natured, intelligent women who came and sat by my bed-
side and seemed to enjoy being there; they told me their stories, often
in detail, their hopes and disappointments. They told me about life in
the hospital and complained about their hours, assignments, and this
supervisor or that. At last I began to sleep fitfully for two or three hours
a night. Sleep deprivation is a torture all right, Amnesty International
says it and so do I. But in fact it didn't have much to do one way or the
other with my recovery, and of course in the hospital I had no work to
do, so it didn't matter whether I could think straight.

Eventually I learned from the nurses, chiefly by letting them talk and not asking questions, what had happened to me or at least some of it. They seemed eager to tell. For one thing, the doctors had loaded me with charcoal, which was supposed to absorb the toxins in the pills I'd taken. No doubt it did; but it also caused me to vomit, which in the nature of the case must have been intended, while at the instant of vomiting I aspirated a sizable amount of the stuff – charcoal – into my lungs, which presumably was not intended. Not until much later, after I had been discharged from the hospital, did I begin to think that those in charge ought to have foreseen this possibility, or even probability, and to have prevented it, which might have been easy. If someone had turned my head toward the side, I might not have breathed in all that junk. But I don't know when or where the charcoal was administered, in the emergency room or the ICU, or even in the ambulance on the way to the hospital. No doubt those people were working as hard as they could and events were occurring rapidly. I don't blame anyone. In effect, however, I ended up with suffocation and radical pneumonia, the latter continuing to be the chief problem after I regained consciousness, not the poisons I had given myself. I've said I suffered no pain, but there was a time – maybe more than once – when the doctor pushed a rod down into my lungs to make me cough. I don't know if this was a pain or not, but it was horrifying, the choking and gasping, the thumping of my heart. It was like being asphyxiated right there and then. I had an impression of the doctor, a stocky man, leaning over me, his knee on the bed, one hand holding down my shoulder, the other pushing this thing in and out of me. It was a rape, it was terrifying, one of the most awful things that has ever happened to me. I remember Ray Carver telling me about the same procedure after his operation for lung cancer. He said it was the worst part of the whole ordeal. In my case it had the desired effect and some of the junk came up. But some stayed down, and until the day I left the hospital the doctors and nurses continued to hear sounds of pneumonia when they listened to me with their ever-present stethoscopes, as they did unrelentingly even after I felt okay and ready to go home.

ONE DOESN'T KNOW, LYING there, how weak one is. Or how awful one looks. On the fifth or sixth day, when I was first permitted to go to the bathroom, I saw my face in the mirror. To get shut of urinals and bedpans was a break, a big one, but the shock of that vision, that apparition in the mirror, was a more than equal shove in the opposite direction. My beard, which I'd worn for more than twenty years, was gone, but I had known that because I'd felt the sharp stubble with my fingers; the nurses had told me it interfered with the tape needed to hold my tubes in the right positions. But what a face was revealed! I had lost weight precipitately, of course, twenty pounds or more; my cheeks were hollow, my eyes much larger than I'd ever seen them, like frog's eyes, and my skin was dark and bruised, covered with tiny hairline creases as if it were tanned cowhide. I looked eighty years old. In fact I looked like my mother when she was eighty-five, paralyzed by stroke and dying. I gaped in revulsion and dismay. Then I became fascinated and stared at myself until the nurse rapped on the door and said loudly, "Are you okay in there?" I flushed the john and walked out and went back to bed. But after that I always studied myself in the bathroom mirror when I could. It was like looking at myself as painted by Dürer or Ivan Albright. It was as close to seeing myself dead as I expect to come.

What had I seen when I had been dead? Not myself, but not much else either. I remember what Carl Jung wrote in his memoirs about the vision that came to him when he was near death, how he had found himself out in space somewhere, near a floating castle, a place of serenity and happiness which he knew would have been his destination; but then his recovery from whatever was wrong with him intervened, and he came back to consciousness. What trivial nonsense! At least it's trivial to me because, although I can't say for a fact that Jung was deceived or was lying, at the same time I can't see what relevance his vision has in the real world, which is the only world. At best it must be a kind of wishful dreaming or hallucinating. A good friend of mine has told me of a similar vision she saw when she was close to death, a vision so in keeping with her benevolent and sensitive character that I believe, myself, it was just an extension of that character. Indeed, if one is conscious at such a time of any perception at all, dream, fantasy, hallucination, or whatever, to my mind it means only that one is not sufficiently dead.

What I saw was blackness. It was neither underground nor in outer space. It was not the darkness of a closed room. It was neither a solid, a fluid, nor an atmosphere. I cannot think of any analogy or metaphor to explain or describe it. It was blackness, nothing else, and it was enclosing me – except that "I" was not there and no action, either of enclosing or any other, occurred. Yet somehow I was aware – aware of the blackness and that it was not quite entirely still. It was composed of indistinguishable particles, perhaps what the ancients meant by atoms, which were in flux, not going anywhere but moving in a slow dance backward and forward. Since I could not "see" this, even inwardly, I don't know how I "knew" it. But no doubt my perception of the movement meant that I was still technically alive, as of course I was, when I arrived at the hospital, even though I exhibited none of the ordinary "vital signs" – breath, pulse, pupillary reflex, etc. My brain was still generating electrical impulses, or doing whatever a brain does. If the motion of the blackness had ceased I would have ceased – entirely – and there would have been neither motion nor blackness nor anything else.

I "remembered" the blackness and its motion when I first became conscious in the ICU. In fact I think the "memory" existed before I became conscious, so that at the very first instant of awakening, or just before that instant, I was "in" the blackness. At any rate it was the first impression I was cognizant of after my going under, and it had the kind of "depth-beyond-time" that dream-reality often has when one remembers it just after waking up. That is, the blackness existed in another "state," which was literally timeless: it could have been a minute, a year, or a century; or it could have been faster than instantaneous, occupying no time at all. Is that eternity? I don't know; I am ignorant of this. Eternity means no more to me now – but certainly no less – than it did when I was five years old and gazed in fear and wonder at the stars. But whereas the idea of "eternity" has always made me unhappy, or at least uncomfortable (which behaviorists say is the same thing), my "memory" of the blackness was not at all uncomfortable but quite the contrary: it was happy. Not in the sense of *ecstatic* as we normally use the term now, meaning sexual or generally appetitive transport, being "out of this world," but rather in the sense of *blissful*, a replete contentedness. It was a state of mind I had never experienced before, and I mean that literally; but it was present in my mind clearly and strongly when I first came to. And it has been present ever since, it has become part of my being. I don't mean that after my suicide the fears, angers, weaknesses, and other obsessive responses of my prior mind did not return; they did, all of them, at times very powerfully. But the sense of strange, new, astounding happiness has remained with me as well.

I was not afraid. I felt no fear whatever. Emphatically. If no "scene" or "vision" appeared to me in the blackness, then nothing to frighten me could be in the blackness either, no conventional sense of the "void," the "beyond," the "mystery." I know this means giving up a notion so dear to even the most hylotheistic imaginations that it seems a stark necessity. The mystery of death has always in every time and place been the most constant element of human feeling, as we know from art and writing, even though it must always be evoked indirectly. Proust gives us a sense of it in the final volume of his huge novel when he writes about soldiers on leave in Paris during the First World War:

> It seemed almost that there was something cruel in these leaves granted to men at the front. When they first came on leave, one said to oneself: "They will refuse to go back, they will desert." And indeed they came not merely from places which seemed to us unreal, because we had only heard them spoken of in the newspapers and could not conceive how a man was able to take part in these titanic battles and emerge with nothing worse than a bruise on his shoulder; it was from the shores of death, whither they would soon return, that they came to spend a few moments in our midst, incomprehensible to us, filling us with tenderness and terror and a feeling of mystery, like phantoms whom we summon from the dead, who appear to us for a second, whom we dare not question, and who could, in any case, only reply: "You cannot possibly imagine."

From "the shores of death," exactly. Even as great a wordspinner as Marcel Proust must resort to cliché. These soldiers have been to those shores and have returned with nothing more than a bruise on the shoulder, meaning that they are men like the rest of us and cannot say anything about their experience of mystery with which we might assuage our tenderness and terror. There is no mystery. Or rather, the mysterious thing about death is that it is not mysterious. Our elemental sense of fitness is appalled by this – death ought to be mysterious – and we are beset by great romantic frustration because it isn't. Well, we are people of the world as it is this minute, the modern world, and as human beings who wish to wear our humanity with a certain grace – though what we really wish is to justify it – we acknowledge our frustration and go on with our lives. Above all we do not ask what we can know. In the ordinary sense of cognition we cannot *know* death any more than we know most other states of existence, such as the mind of a newborn infant or a dinosaur, or even the fullness of our own minds in their commonest moments, walking along a street of our hometown, tying our shoes, etc.

This was how I felt in the hospital. And although my image in the mirror was shocking, repulsive, peculiarly fascinating, and took some time to adjust to, my happiness was not diminished. I was high – and not from the oxygen either. I was high on life, my recovered life, even though "life" for me at that time was thoroughly elemental. I couldn't go anywhere or do anything. I could hardly think. I don't remember any mental activity that wasn't involuntary. But the animal in me was responding to this remarkable turn of events like the rabbit that is dropped unaccountably from the eagle's talons. I was alive. I had been happy when I was dead and now I was happy when I was alive. It had nothing to do with thought, but only with sensory experience, touching my own arm or belly, swallowing, excreting, being touched by the nurses, listening to the music in my head. I carried on presumably intelligent conversations with nurses and eventually with visitors, but only in a kind of academic autonomia, my tongue still running – like a cartoon character running in the air above a chasm   from the impetus of the classroom; or maybe I was talking nonsense, babbling uncontrollably, and the nurses and visitors were too kind to tell me so. I talked to everyone, doctors, nurses, aides and technicians, the young woman who mopped the floor of my room and told me about her 1965 Mustang and gave me copies of *Road and Track* to read, without the least discomposure. I was manic, I suppose, though I don't care for clinical language. "Carruth," I said to myself, "you are experiencing exactly the conditions you have all your life and in all your acute and chronic psychopathology feared *more* than death, being in a hospital, locked up, among total strangers, no way to escape, nothing to quell the scream bubbling in your throat." Yet I felt none of the anxiety that had destroyed large parts of my life during the sixty-six years before I ended up in the ICU.

A LOT OF PEOPLE are talking about rebirth nowadays. It's the fundamentalist fad in these last years of the old millennium. Apocalyptic behavior is to be expected, we are told. And all of us are sometimes fundamentalists, all of us who take the trouble – and trouble is what it is – to face "ultimate reality" from time to time. I don't know about being reborn in the exuberance of an evangelical camp meeting, but if it's anything like being reborn in an ICU, it's wonderful. And it lasts a long time. Not that such a course as mine can be recommended; it obviously can't. Nor can it be faked; near suicides and theatrical suicides, perhaps compulsive suicides of any kind, won't work. One has to have a clear and resolute intent to die, which apparently everyone agrees – medical doctors, psychiatrists, friends – was the case with me.

Of course everyone agreed I was crazy, too. Doctors are by profession devoted to life and to saving life; for them to believe that suicide can be anything but insanity, at least in ordinary American middle-class life, would require them to be crazy themselves. And of all people who are not crazy the most not crazy are doctors. In their world this is axiomatic. So there I was, surrounded by doctors, under the control of doctors, my life and being regulated by doctors, and though they were kind enough to pretend they thought I was rational, especially after friends pointed out to them that I was a "professor" – I dislike the word myself – and a somewhat well-known writer, it was understood by everyone that I really was crazy and that my friends were as well. Consequently, when it came time for me to be discharged from the ICU, the doctors would let me go only with the proviso that I pass immediately into the laughing academy, the hatchery, the local asylum. I had no choice; I was still too weak to dress myself and walk out the way heroes do in the movies. But even then, when I had agreed to their condition, two days more were required – at better than $1,000 a day – to negotiate the terms and methods of transfer from one hospital to another, so that both hospitals could have in writing, certified and attested, exactly the point at which one hospital's responsibility ended and the other's began. Perhaps this was partly impelled by fear of legal liability, which we know has become a grave enough problem for medical people in recent years; but I believe the doctors would have behaved the same even if no question of legal liability had been posed. I was a suicide and I was crazy, and that was the end of it. The result was that eventually I was taken from one hospital to the other, a journey of about an hour and a half between two cities, in a locked ambulance with two burly young men to attend me and with impressive receipts and delivery invoices signed by both parties when I was handed – which is the precise word – from the locked vehicle to the door of the locked loony bin.

I could have protested. If I had done it vigorously enough, I could have succeeded. Legally, I was not a certifiable nut, was still responsible for myself. But in such circumstances who has the strength for that? Not only the doctors but friends and family, having been "counseled" by the doctors, all believed I must go to the psychiatric hospital. I had made phone calls to friends who were shrinks, and they said the same thing. Everyone said the same thing, without exception, so what was I to do? I was the only one who knew that the hatch was the wrong place for me. But though I knew this – partly because I had spent a long time in the hatch thirty-five years earlier in a vain attempt to deal with my psychoneurotic anxiety – and knew also that what I really needed was to go home and relax, the truth was that I didn't have a home, and I knew this too, knew it well, with the consequence that I didn't protest and found myself in a locked ward with a number of people who were hollering or banging the walls or walking around full of Haldol, stiff, jerky, headed for tardive dyskinesia, God help them. On the other hand this was not a hospital that treated violent mental illness; I got out of the locked ward and onto an open ward after about three days, and I remained in the hospital only two weeks altogether. Not a bad hitch compared to the fifteen months I had served thirty-five years before.

And I was happy the whole time. Happy as a clam, and for the same reasons: I was alive, more or less comfortable, protected. But the chief reason was being alive. Again, as in the ICU, I talked to everyone, made friends with nearly all the other patients on the ward, about forty people, plus scores of staff workers of every description. I told them little about myself but listened to account after account of their personal miseries, including the complaints of injustice at the hands of the hospital administration heard again and again from nurses, aides, and technicians, and I attended scores of "group therapy" sessions, which were a farce when they weren't a persecution, making people cry, etc., especially the women, young and old, and one noted that nearly all the group leaders were men, even the leaders of the special "women's group" – what could be more ridiculous? – though when I asked one of the women if she wasn't affronted by this, she said, "No." Also it's worth noting that of the forty-odd people on the ward, only two of us were men, and even if for unknown reasons these numbers were extreme at that particular time, I can't believe the disparity isn't significant.

At the same time many changes for the better had been introduced since the last time I'd been an inmate. For one, the hospital had no shock room; the few patients for whom electroshock was prescribed were taken to another hospital, and no one ever suggested it for me. (I had had a series of ten shocks in 1954, which were no help at all.) For another, all of us had ready access to the phone. Our outgoing mail was not read by doctors. Two days after I was admitted a person from an independent legal organization came and informed me of my rights, including the right to dispute and I think interdict any medications I thought were wrongly prescribed, and he gave me a printed leaflet confirming my legal status. All this was markedly different from my earlier immurement, when one could not make free contact with anybody outside the institution, certainly not a lawyer. Moreover I was not now subjected to any of the foolish treatments I had had to undergo formerly: "hydrotherapy" (in which one stood naked in a tiled stall while being battered by two cold and high-powered jets of water), "occupational therapy" (making belts and neckties), or "physical therapy" (though I could volunteer for exercise classes if I wished – I did – and a weight-lifting room was provided for younger people). But the greatest change is in the length of time one is expected to stay. Earlier I had spent a year and a quarter in the hospital and had known others who had been confined for many years, but now of the forty-odd people on the ward only three or four had been in the hospital for more than a month and most were discharged in two or three weeks. On other wards, such as those for people addicted to drugs or alcohol or with eating disorders, the expected time until discharge was longer, and there may have been wards I was unaware of. But I saw only one patient who was a chronic long-time loser, an elderly senile woman who was said to have been in psychiatric hospitals since she was seventeen. She spent her days in a reclining chair in the lounge, talking unintelligibly to herself and making strange angry noises. Nothing could be done for her. It struck me that she was there more to furnish an example – edifying without doubt – for the rest of us than for any benefit to herself.

This lounge, in fact, was the greatest discomfort in the hatch. It was the only place where smoking was permitted. It was also the only place where a television set was turned on from six in the morning until midnight. Dozens of times a day I was up against the choice of a cigarette with MTV or the smokeless quiet of my room. Not much of a discomfort

perhaps. Even less, considering that most of the time I could find some-
one to talk with in the lounge, someone who would join me in facing
away from the tube and ignoring its racket. We were not permitted to
have lighters – the institute has not changed in this – but an electric
lighter, similar to a car lighter but with a fine wire mesh across the front
of it, was fixed on the wall and could be made to glow by pressing a but-
ton. Most of the patients were smokers – the opposite proportion to
that outside; let the Surgeon General make of it what he will – with the
result that hundreds of times a day, perhaps thousands, someone would
walk into the lounge with a cigarette ready, go up to the button and
press it, then lean close to the lighter to get the smoke going. It was rit-
ualistic. Kissing the wall is what we called it.

"Hey Jim, you going to kiss the wall?"

"Damn right."

Well, I was there two weeks, as I've said. I went to a fair number of
group therapy sessions, took many psychological tests, was inter-
viewed by various doctors and other people, saw a psychiatrist who had
been assigned to me for fifteen minutes each day, went out several times
with groups in a big Dodge van to visit parks on the outskirts of the city,
and toward the end went out with friends to dinner. I was mildly scared
a couple of times when younger patients got into a fracas. I was irritated
late at night when I couldn't sleep and the nurse in charge wouldn't
authorize anyone to open the lounge (locked from midnight until six
o'clock) and let me smoke, though sometimes, inconsistently, this was
permitted. But mostly I was happy. Not only that, I was cheerful. This
is confirmed in the "report" that was written on my case, which I was
given to read after my discharge and which summarized the immense
file that had accumulated in only two weeks, hundreds and hundreds of
observations by doctors, nurses, technicians, aides, and who knows
how many others, plus data from physical and psychological tests of
many kinds. It was a file three inches thick – what an expense of paper!
The report said I was outgoing, good-humored, etc. – not my usual self
at all, not a pessimist, skeptic, and grump. I was a *new man*. Exactly.

Seeing my psychiatrist once a day in the hospital, incidentally, was
another change from earlier, when I had been lucky to see a doctor once
a week. I can't say the psychiatrist assigned to me in Syracuse, Veena
Kayastha, who is a wise and magnanimous woman from India, taught
me anything I hadn't known before – after all my years in psychotherapy

this would have been unlikely – but she changed the angle of vision from which I looked at myself; and this was indispensable. I have continued to see her, though less and less frequently, since being discharged from the hospital.

IN MANY OF THE GROUP sessions the question came up of the acute embarrassment most suicidal patients feel before friends and relatives afterward, and of the hindrance a history of suicide may be, once it gets on the record, to finding a job. Many patients on the ward were suicidals, I'd guess more than half, ranging from high school girls, fresh and pretty and naive, to people my age or older; some were longtime repeaters. When one of the group leaders asked me how I felt about this, I said, "Well, in my line of work it's more an advantage than a disadvantage." By this time nearly everyone knew I was a poet. So my remark got a laugh, and a laugh was by no means a bad thing in that place, though the group leaders often didn't think so: they'd look annoyed and then right away put on a false smile and get back to the serious business of making somebody squirm. I became annoyed with their implacable Rotarian optimism and formulism, their essentially authoritarian methods – they always knew best – and their moral impeccability. Once I tried to suggest that attitudes toward suicide are relative and derive from diverse cultural sources. Social, religious, and ethnic factors are variable. We all know about the spy who keeps a dose of cyanide in his ring so he can do away with himself when the going gets rough. A fictional stereotype; yet I have no doubt he exists in reality. Even in our Christian culture, which since the days of the early church has regarded suicide as a sin, most people would agree that someone facing extreme physical torture ought to have the choice of taking his or her own life. In Japan a politician who has failed in office is expected to retire, not to his estate in the country, but to the next room, where he sticks himself with a horrid big knife. This is the honorable thing to do. For centuries in India a new widow, even if she was still in her teens, was expected to commit suttee – to cast herself on her husband's pyre. Again it was the honorable thing to do, no matter how sexist and stupid. I wonder if Christianity may not be the only prominent religion which proscribes suicide categorically as sinful, i.e., denies suicides a burial in the common, consecrated graveyard. At any rate, attitudes toward suicide vary. Even in our ordinary American social cross section, attitudes toward suicide are more variable than the doctors care to admit. For that matter, doctors themselves have a higher suicide rate than many other professions, perhaps – who knows? – right up there next to the priests.

I have had three close friends who died of the same kind of cancer within the past year. One of them lingered longer in the final stage than the others, and everyone agrees that the latter were the luckier. Death for them was a blessing. In fact this feeling has become so commonplace with respect to victims of cancer that we scarcely wince any more when we express it. The sooner one dies the better.

Some years ago I had a friend whose domestic life was in a shambles. Part of the trouble was not his doing, but he was so bound up, so repressed and inhibited, that he could talk to no one, either psychiatrist or friend, about it. He was forty-five years old, had three minor children, was a success in his work, a liked and respected person. He went into the woods and shot himself. I had to go with the search party – cops with dogs mostly – the next day; when we found him I had to identify him. It was awful. Anyone could have told him that what he should do was forget the whole mess and go to California; this is the common, effective American expedient. He was simply incapable of this. Incapable. In such a case can anyone say with certainty that his suicide was wrong?

The idea of suicide makes everyone shudder, even those who have done it. It's the *frisson* we feel when we encounter the nonbeing we carry inside us, when somebody, as we say, walks over our grave. Perhaps this is why we make excuses for suicide, excusing ourselves in the potential future. John Donne, who was as rigorously devout in his later years as anyone could be, in his *Biathanatos* excuses religiously motivated suicides, against the teaching of the church. Indeed, almost every philosopher has discussed suicide in one work or another because the topic is obviously, almost conveniently, close to the heart of all moral problems. The most famous example in our time is Albert Camus in *The Myth of Sisyphus.*

I've always thought that if we must have capital punishment – and I don't for a minute accept the necessity – the Athenians invented the best, most humane method when they gave Socrates the cup of hemlock and let him administer it to himself. At that same time not far away the

Macedonians, Spartans, Israelites, and others were hacking at people with axes or roasting them over fires or nailing them to crosses. For that matter who today would not, if allowed to do so, choose suicide over hanging, electrocution, or the gas chamber, no matter how "painless" these methods may be? Irrational, yes. But when an inevitability has been established, presuming philosophically that all inevitabilities are in themselves and of necessity unjust, at some point the human being then wishes to choose it, to make it his or her election, even in the case of the death sentence, as if to ratify not only the injustice but his or her own autonomy by acting in the semblance of freedom. Whether or not this makes good sense, it is good psychology.

Suicide has been chosen by many and all kinds of people, including many writers. Off the top of my head I think of Lindsay, Mayakovsky, Yesenin, Teasdale, Virginia Woolf, Crane, Hemingway, F. O. Matthiessen, Kees, Cesare Pavese (that most vigorous of poets), Berryman, Jarrell, Plath, Sexton.... And painters too: Van Gogh, Mark Rothko. Again and again they do it, many different people for many different reasons. And is anyone able to say that all these people are wrong?

Some say that suicide is against nature. This is the "faith" of the doctors, I think. All nature strives to live, is what they say, the survival of the fittest, *elan vital*, etc. But in the first place this is wrong. Among some species it is death to copulate, but they copulate anyway. Among others a parent will give up her own life for the sake of her young. Among still others individuals who are old or diseased cause their own deaths, or conspire in them. And in the second place it doesn't matter what nature does. What matters is the human mind and spirit, as I assume I need not argue.

My own mind and spirit became filled, during the time in question, with happiness, as I have said. It was a peculiar feeling, something like the high I experienced in the ICU during my all-night, internal jam sessions, and I can't say enough about the excitement of that. I've been playing the blues all my life, sometimes on musical instruments but, like most musicians, even more often in my head, yet I never knew another time when I felt the exhilaration I felt that night. I was flying; my whole body was buzzing and writhing; though I was too weak to walk, almost too weak to raise my head, I was incandescent with energy; and I believed – but who can tell? – that my musical imagination was soaring in extraordinary new inventions. I was drugged? Maybe. I don't know what was flowing into me through those tubes, except for the oxygen, and my experience of drugs otherwise (except for alcohol) has been limited. But I can't believe (1) that I could achieve so high a high or (2) that I could perceive and remember it so clearly if I were merely intoxicated. And this was the feeling, this happiness, that I felt, varying in intensity, all the time in both hospitals and continue to feel to this day. A feeling of frothiness in my head, of effervescence. It is like falling in love ten times, successively but not simultaneously and with no other person implicated. The happiness is generated entirely within myself and directed entirely back to myself.

Yet the knowledge of it is shareable.

Is this what St. Theresa felt? For pages I've been skirting the idea of mystical experience; I've used the word spiritual and have alluded to rebirth. I suspect that in its sensational manifestation my happiness is indeed close to religious ecstasy. But at the same time I've been a back-country Yankee pragmatist and cynic all my life, and I cling to this conviction still, not only because it seems to my mind, which has been drawn to the question since I was a child, to be right, but because it is one of the very few continuities in my life that can hold thought and experience and feeling, my personality, together. I do not believe at all that a contradiction exists between my happiness and my rationalism. I resist to the end – this is part of the clinging – my friends who smile and say, "Well, we knew you'd come round to god at last." God has nothing to do with it, if only because he or she is in my view functionally nonexistent, an abstraction with no power and no intelligence. And no mystery; the mystery is within oneself, at the bottommost pit of oneself, and to call this a god is to commit suicide in a more drastic and distraught way than I ever contemplated with my mere overdose. It is to give up one's humanity, which is precisely our being not godly, our incapacity. Elsewhere I have argued for the notion that spiritual and mystical experience are different.[2] The mystic is someone who has immediate knowledge of supernatural power. This has never happened to me; all the hallucinatory incidents in my life can be convincingly explained by rational means. (Of course, this does not at all preclude

---

[2] "The Act of Love: Poetry and Personality," *Working Papers* (Athens: University of Georgia Press, 1982), p. 219.

mystical knowledge in other minds; it does not even preclude the fact of this in my own mind. I have a friend who is a painter, for instance, and when she is stumped by a problem in her work, Picasso tells her what to do by means of messages transmitted through a pencil held in her left, nonwriting hand. I believe what she says. But nothing remotely like this has ever happened to me.) Spiritual, as distinct from mystical, knowledge is all knowledge of the human spirit in its surpassing of material cause in Aristotle's sense of the word. The human spirit is human, grounded in our bodies, but it is still spirit. Spirituality is an extension of materiality, in the same sense that love is a refinement of sex, but is no less spiritual for that. The differences between spiritual and esthetic experience, or between either of them and emotional experience, are too abstruse for discussion in this essay, but to my mind, briefly, these differences entail discriminations among states or levels of feeling and have more to do with the way the feelings are evoked or produced than with their intrinsic qualities.

Is this a cynical view? It is necessary to bear in mind that cynicism does not mean merely a sardonic attitude toward life, love, or any other value, although this is what the word most often signifies in ordinary discourse. My dictionary says: "The Cynics [in ancient philosophy] taught that virtue is the only good, and that its essence lies in self-control and independence." It is easy to put too much stock in self-control and independence, as some cynics have, which results in a kind of puritanism; but it is equally easy to dismiss them altogether, which results in quietism. For me virtue is indeed the only good. Self-control and independence are the states of being toward which I strive continually, acknowledging that I'm damned lucky to attain either of them for even a moment.

And luck has a good deal to do with virtue, and with self-control and independence, too. Any artist knows this. A poet or painter must work in exceptional and solitary diligence to sustain technique and the required pliancy of imagination, that is, to keep the artistic apparatus in a state of readiness for the stroke of luck that alone can materialize a genuine work of art when it comes; more than this, the artist must not only work but live in a state of devotion to things greater than himself. But no dereliction from hard work and devotion is implied in deferring to luck. Deference is a recognition of reality, what Wallace Stevens called "the necessary angel," who must mediate the imaginative procedure. A work of art – a work of virtue – is luck welcomed and accepted, the success of chance. And happiness is the feeling that goes with it. What I mean to say is that happiness itself is not virtue, in spite of the official American philosophy to the contrary, but it is the feeling that accompanies virtue. Often it's the feeling of being lucky.

The example may seem crass to some, but not to realists. happiness is winning the lottery. Everyone knows this. The guy who goes to bed with a million dollars more than he had when he got up is happy without a doubt. (It's a fact that the words *happen* and *happiness* both come from the root *hap*, which means chance.) Money is not everything, and for those of us who are serious about virtue it is not even much; we would rather produce a fine poem or painting than a fat bank account. Some of us would even rather produce a good action in the world. And we believe that our feeling when we do these things is happier by far than the gambler's mere rapture. In my case the happiness I've been speculating about came from the luck of being alive. And what is being alive at all if it isn't luck, whether good luck or bad? At any moment in our lives we know we might never have existed; our conception, that obscure beginning, was the extreme fortuity – chance as the absolute foundation – and awareness of this stays with us always. My suicide was a reminder of it, as my recovery was a resumption. I don't believe I experienced rebirth, which can come only from an unimaginable reconception and in effect would be a second origin – a contradiction in terms. Each of us has only one origin, one fundamental piece of luck (good or bad). In my suicide I experienced a *renewal* of luck. And I believe that because I was an artist, a person who had devotion and worked in discipline, I was ready for that renewal and for its reward in happiness.

WHY WORRY IT LIKE THIS? What is this need to understand and explain? My luck was not a change of knowledge but of vision. My happiness was not a state of doing but of being. Why not accept what had been given to me and be grateful and let it alone? This is what many of my friends – and especially those who are artists – would recommend.

I can only say that acceptance without questioning is contrary to my nature. The urgency in me – in my mind, my soul – is precisely to understand and explain. When I am presented with a gift, my impulse is to examine it, to look it in the mouth. How else can one appreciate it? How else can one arrive at an estimation of value, of moral and esthetic quality? In sessions of group therapy at the hospital I was accused of being too intellectual; both the staff and my fellow patients thought my responses to questions were too abstract and buried the essential feeling or instinct in an array of complication. I've been used to this all my life. The only thing to do when it happens is shut up, which is what I pretty much did, in the hospital as elsewhere. But I felt violated. Everything I know as writer and critic, everything I know about poetry and life, tells me that the effort to analyze a feeling makes that feeling stronger, not weaker. Likewise with a poem, painting, or piece of music. At the same time any effort to suppress or circumvent one's own intelligence leads to self-rebuke and depression. As my friend Paul Goodman used to say, I can't be any stupider than I am. But I should add that for me analysis is rather close to what I think other people mean by meditation.

The *recognition* of these things – the *lucid* recognition, as Camus would say – is important to me. And this too has to do with vision.

ANOTHER WAY TO LOOK at happiness and luck is under the rubric of time – the way people always look at it. True luck is not money but time, additional time: ask any veteran of Vietnam. Not one of them would take a million dollars for the extraordinary luck that brought them through alive. Poets and theologians have insisted from the beginning that happiness is an escape from time, human time, either through a life after death or, before death, through an experience of spiritual communion or mystical or esthetic transport. But a third way, as mythology attests, is to die and come back to life. This is the meaning in Western culture of the descent to the underworld, from Inanna to Dante. If one dies, then one's life is ended, meaning that the human computation of time, which is imposed on us by death, has ended, has been, as people say, terminated or wiped out. If one comes back from death then one must either begin a new life, which is impossible because all the defining elements of one's personality have already been established, or one must live in a new, different computation of time. Can one die twice? Of course; no human being has ever returned to life without eventually dying again. (The gods were always jealous and hard-nosed on that score.) This seems to mean that one's new computation of time would be imposed by one's new forthcoming death, however near or remote, and that in consequence this new computation is not much different from the old one. This is the logic of it. But the psychology of it, the spirituality of it, is another matter. One's inner intuitive organ of cognizance knows that dead is dead; but it cannot know the distinction between all-but-dead and dead. That is to say, one's inner intuitive organ of cognizance cannot accommodate itself to the idea of dying twice. If one all-but-dies, then the awareness of time as a human computation dies too, and the new, regained time when one returns is uncomputed.

This is what people call "borrowed time" or even "stolen time," which are mere folkifications, a common irrational wish-fulfillment. From whom or what could one possibly borrow or steal it? No, uncomputed time is much closer to what is called "free time," in both the sense of time with which one may do what one chooses and of time that is given without the normal payment, which is death. It is time outside the ordinary understanding of succession. And what I mean by "the ordinary understanding of succession" is precisely the imposed computation of one's lifetime under the pressure of predictable death that I have pointed to in the last paragraph. Free time is what Proust was talking about when he said that a remembered sensation in its sensory immediacy but temporal remoteness gives one an experience outside of normal chronology. It is the time that Alice found when she popped down the rabbit hole. It is the time that old people find when they fall in love, a release or reprieve from the predicted progression of sexuality-to-impotence-to-senility-to-death; Ford Madox Ford gave us a wonderful picture of this in his poem called "Heaven," and it was no accident that he chose – or more likely acceded to – the metaphor of an afterlife to represent the state of erotic gratification in old age. But in all these cases – Proust's, Alice's, and Ford's – the free time was acquired through complicated procedures entailing extra-personal agents or events. My free time, on the other hand, has come essentially from the experience of death, which is as inward and personal as any experience can be. In this my experience is like the mystic's, though the mystic would probably say that his or her experience is on the contrary as outward and impersonal as any experience could be, thus raising the question, which is unanswerable, of whether the utterly inward and utterly outward may not be the same thing.

All of which seems to mean that the luckiest kind of luck is that which gives one free time or time-outside-of-time. Moreover it is that which occurs solely within consciousness and with no reference to any externality whatever. Hence it goes without saying, at least in the terms of this essay, that this is what gives one the greatest happiness. One could achieve it by catching Alzheimer's disease and then arresting it just at the stage before complete loss of self-consciousness; one could achieve it in ways I have never thought of and would be unlikely to imagine. But one way to achieve it is by all-but-dying, and probably, though I see no way to demonstrate it, the degree of happiness resulting will be in direct ratio to the nearness of one's approach to death. One of my doctors remarked that my attempt at suicide had been "lethal," and it was clear from the context that this was meant literally. (The dictionary: "*lethal* is applied to that which by its very nature is bound to cause death or which exists for the purpose of destroying life.") So my luck, my unintentional discovery of time-outside-time, has been great indeed, and, leaving aside questions of possible brain damage or other physical impairments, so has been my happiness.

A FURTHER CONSIDERATION arises under the heading of identity, which is, heaven knows, a hackneyed enough refrain in the literature of my time, both fictional and clinical. I won't pursue it here. But it's worth mentioning that during my whole life prior to my suicide I had never been able to identify any part of my ego that might be central to the rest or that functioned in a way beyond the mere response to external stimuli. Among writers this is called style or voice. When I was young and under the influence of W. B. Yeats, I believed I knew his voice so well that if a new poem turned up purporting to be by him, I could tell right away, simply by reading the lines aloud to myself, whether the claim was genuine. But I could never find so distinct a voice in my own work, which instead seemed a disconcerting concatenation of voices, other people's voices mimicked or faked, including in some poems the voice of Yeats himself. This is a matter of perception, of course, and other people tell me that no matter how many *personae* appear in my poems, they recognize in the language, the thought, and the feeling a consistent personality. I hope they're right, but I don't know if they are. What is important here is that I discovered in suicide a way to unify my sense of self, the sense which had formerly been so refracted and broken up. This will seem bizarre to many of my friends, including my students. The truth is, however, that the practice of writing poetry, to which I have given a lifetime, has always seemed to me suspect, not quite legitimate, while suicide is without doubt an action in the world, something that one has done or not done, really and objectifiably. This is what I am. This is my identity, whatever anyone may think of it. Suicide is not only what I did but what I was capable of doing. Elemental though it may be, it still gives shape, integrity, and a certain fullness to the figure of myself – minuscule, of course – that I see out there in history. It isn't much, but it's more than I had before. And this is a real and significant feeling in me, no matter how other people may recoil from it, as I myself would have recoiled if it had been presented to me in my ante-suicidal ignorance.

AT ANY POINT IN this discussion, but particularly at this one, the question is whether my suicide was a mistake. I see no way to answer in terms of what had happened before the suicide. I'd had a long run of bad luck, no doubt of that, precluding the possibility of virtue, at least in my private life. But exactly how bad was it? And how bad must it be to justify suicide? We have no measurement. The church is right, from its standpoint, in making a blanket rejection, because even if absolute objective criteria could be found, which they can't, they could never be applied reasonably in individual cases. When you and I have been infected by the same flu bug, do we suffer equal pain? No, evidently we don't. But beyond this, the crudest observation, we can't say much about our relative qualities and quantities of pain, any more than we can about other elements of our relative subjectivities, including our need for suicide. All one can say in this respect is that *at some point* suicide may become feasible in anyone's life. This is not saying much, and it doesn't satisfy our need for something conclusive in such a difficult moral predicament. We are left where we, as mundane and imperfect human beings, always are.

But in terms of what followed after the suicide, I don't see how anyone, even the doctors, can maintain it was a mistake except in fare-thee-well doctrinairian terms, which I reject on every ground.

Another point: my suicide occurred at a moment in life when death would not have been ill-timed. I had done about as much as one is normally expected to do. This doesn't mean I had no obligations still outstanding; at any point in anyone's life responsibility is always present; but I had generally done what I could. In my writing I had concluded my best work some years earlier. Even in teaching, which for me was in any case a late development and not something that could be called professional, any time at which one chooses to depart is as appropriate as any other. Teaching is like working on the assembly line of an auto factory; the semesters go past, one applies an air wrench here, a soldering gun there; but the task is repetitive and can be interrupted with equal felicity or infelicity at any point. Hence in every sector, disregarding the fortuity of what has happened afterward, my death at the moment of my suicide would have been as opportune as anyone's.[3]

If my suicide was a mistake, it was such a mistake as is a part of life. Suicide in this respect is like any death, a part of the experience of living, consequent upon one's original luck. It is something existing within the potentiality of life. Is this possibility of suicide therefore a reason for suicide? That's a conundrum. Given a sufficiently anxious sensibility, it might be. But our proclivity for mistakes is not a reason for not living. What I'm saying here is that suicide is a choice, a free act. Whether a mistake or not, whether it succeeds or not, it authenticates the freedom of the intelligent being who chooses it. It is a powerful indicator of our relevance to ourselves as human beings. We can and do choose whether to live or to die. Granted, the Mickey Mouse psychologists who are trying to legislate morality on this question and others – e.g., in the public schools – decline such a view of suicide and in general try to exclude as much dangerous human freedom as possible, but these people, these technologists of behavior, are anathema to me, just as my own freedom – to choose and to do other things – is crucially important to me. This does not mean I am in favor of what the papers call "teenage suicide," incidentally. Young people must be taught to think. Whenever

---

[3] All this, and indeed the whole essay, applies only to suicide in its relationship to the individual who resorts to it. Scores of good friends were grieved and angered by my action. And what shall I say about the pain inflicted on my two children, who, though grown up and out in the world, are still close to me? This is not only another consideration, it is a different topic.

they are inculcated with such Rotarianized precepts as "respect for life" and the "American way," from sea to shining sea, etc., their capacity for thought is diminished proportionately and in most cases irrevocably. This is not exactly relevant here, but it's important nevertheless.

Alfred Alvarez in his first-rate book about suicide[4] says at the end: "It [suicide] seems to me to be somehow as much beyond social or psychic prophylaxis as it is beyond morality, a terrible but utterly natural reaction to the strained, narrow, unnatural necessities we sometimes create for ourselves." Yes, it is natural. But I think Alvarez takes too much onto himself in this, too much guilt for the "necessities" that summoned his will to suicide. I assume this is an extension of his guilt in other things as well. My own experience is different. The pain suffered beforehand for sixty years was not created by me. It was forced, jammed, crammed, wreaked upon me by… by "Fate," and my decision to kill myself was a decision made in defeat. I no longer had enough strength to carry on, and I mean physical strength as well as emotional and spiritual strength. This happens. Though I had not brutalized myself, I was exhausted from years of brutalization; and exhaustion, as everyone knows, is what old age does: it steals one's endurance. So the suffering is what must be emphasized, without self-pity, the suffering of everyone. It can be documented. "Listen to the newborn infant's cry in the hour of birth – see the death struggles in the final hour – and then declare whether what begins and ends in this way can be intended to be enjoyment." So wrote Søren Kierkegaard, and it's the commonest human sentiment of all. Defeat. My students and people who read my poems will be discouraged or even angered by what I'm saying here. "Look at all those books he wrote. Can that be a defeat?" If it isn't a defeat, it's an irrelevance. One cannot live in the past. Nostalgia is an illness and a delusion. Nor can one live on one's former accomplishments, which belong fundamentally to other people. But beyond this, every artist of the second half of the twentieth century knows that his or her working life is in at least one sense a resounding defeat, for what understanding or explanation or solace can art bring to a people who are like animals being driven up the ramp to the abattoir and who know that their imminent, massive deaths are extraneous to any motion of

---

4 A. Alvarez, *The Savage God: A Study of Suicide* (London: Weidenfeld and Nicolson, 1971; New York: Random House, 1972), p. 237.

human mentality whatever? Can poetry, painting, or music overcome the "greenhouse effect"? People will say a society that neglects its arts and artists will be impoverished, but this society is so impoverished already – and from hundreds of quite other causes – that the neglect of art can't make the situation any worse. Artists know this. They know that if they work simply for themselves, or even for some abstract ideal of Art, they and their work will become attenuated and parched. They yearn to be connected. But they can't be, and they are defeated; they are in a condition of unending degradation.

At least in small ways, however, connection is still possible. Since my recovery my good luck has continued. In fact some nearly unbelievably lucky things have happened. One result is that the house I had bought a few months before my suicide, an alien, cold, unfriendly place at the time, has now become a real home. Another is that I am planning to be married soon to a beautiful and loving woman. My life has changed completely, in other words, and in ways I literally could not have believed possible at the time of my suicide and that anyone would have thought extremely unlikely. Moreover I have been welcomed back to my university on a semiretired basis and apparently am teaching as well as ever. As we say, I'm *lucky to be alive*. But the most important result of my new luck is that I am enabled to perform acts of virtue once more. I have moved out of the isolation and alienation of my former life and back into the world, which is where acts of virtue occur. Because of this I am a better writer, whatever the artistic quality of my work from now on may be. Writing is first of all a way of being in the world, a functioning nub of relatedness. Hence my happiness, that frothy feeling, is now with me almost all the time. Bad luck and unhappiness are what I remember from the time before, as they are what I see continually around me in the smaller and larger worlds. Like anyone else, I pay attention to the news. Nor am I foolish enough to think that bad luck and unhappiness may not return to me. I've reached the time of life when one's friends begin shuffling away, usually in pain and humiliation, and saying good-bye is a sorrow I find simply overwhelming; yet it is not incompatible with my happiness. I do what I can, everything I can, so that other people may have good luck and may know it when they do, and in this I'm an average decent sort of a guy. Not that it amounts to much; a few friends, a few students, a few strangers – one cannot hope to reach more. The many kinds of impotence, like the many mistakes, are a part of life. But I am happy even so, happy with my luck and my knowledge of it, with my virtue and the good I can do if I am strong enough.

This is what is important, surely. Happiness, this spiritual happiness, can and does come to people like me – the cynics, as I have called us – so that spirituality is as much a dimension of our pragmatic lives as it is of the exalted lives of the mystics. Maybe I haven't explained it, and maybe no one can. In investigating the expressiveness of a sonnet by Shakespeare one brings to bear every resource one possesses of language, psychology, and thought, thereby increasing one's understanding and pleasure, but in the end one's resources will be exhausted and one's understanding will run into the mystery of the poem. Not a mystery in the sense of an enigma, but in the sense of an unclassifiability. The poem is unique; it cannot be interpreted in any terms but its own, which means that no computer, let it be programmed ever so sophisticatedly, can discover or record all the combinations of nuance that make the poem. The same with personality. The same with my happiness and its spirituality. Yet these, like the poem, exist. I can identify them and believe in them, and believe in the connections they have made for me, as in the hospital when I began, after a lifetime of anxious withdrawal, to talk spontaneously with those around me, performing little acts of virtue. It is a connectedness that has continued. It becomes greater. And the feeling of happiness, which of course I do accept and for which I am truly grateful, is undeniable. It makes all the difference.

Footnote to Suicide

PEOPLE WHO COMMIT suicide and survive are defensive about it. Afterward they say either "I didn't mean to do it," signifying their savoir faire, or "I did mean to do it," signifying their seriousness. In either case they are uneasy. On one hand they don't want to be thought crazy; on the other they don't want to be thought frivolous or half-hearted. The latter is the case with me. I really meant it and when I arrived at the emergency room I was clinically dead. So when I refer to the event I always say that I committed suicide, not that I attempted suicide.

Nevertheless I survived. A fluke. And now I have survived for seven years more, seven years quite unlike and much better than the years before – and I believe this is often true in such cases. Something is to be said, though obviously not much, for the idea that everyone ought to commit suicide once in a while.

Not long after I got out of the hospital I wrote an essay about my experience of death. It was published in a magazine, and since then had been republished in another of my books. And it belongs properly in this sequence of autobiographical fragments. The piece was not an attempt to justify what I had done, since that is impossible, but simply to describe what had happened to me in the suicide itself and its aftermath, and to say what I could about the topic generally. But what is most noticeable to me now about that essay is its unmistakable air of self-love, almost egomania. The whole piece is centered on my interior node of consciousness, however you define that, to the exclusion of nearly everything else. And perhaps that is the basic thing about suicide. Whether temporarily or not, people who commit suicide are totally self-involved – at least that's true of people who commit suicide impetuously, as most do; other cases, in which people give themselves euthanasia, for whatever reason, may be different.

Fragments of Autobiography: Second Series

JUST AS MOST PEOPLE cannot see how someone may be an Eroticist without being a Romanticist so they apparently cannot understand that a poet may have lived in the country most of his life and may have written about "nature" repeatedly, even compulsively, without being a Nature Poet, Farmer Poet, Transcendental Poet, or whatever.

This is the question that is asked of me continually. Not usually in so many words, but it recurs again and again one way or another.

I've been moved to wonder by things in nature that are wonderful, to fear by things terrifying, to curiosity and to fascination by things interesting, but I have not been moved to faith.

I like Charlie Simic's division of the ways of thought and being, of being-in-thought, into three: the Greek, which is Cosmic; the Hebrew, which is Historical; and the Romantic, which is late-eighteenth-century and Transcendental (Sentimental). To them I might add a fourth, the Existential, except that I think this is probably a return to the Cosmic. And the Cosmic way of being-in-thought is solitary. That is, it springs from a consideration of the individual consciousness vis-à-vis reality, from an awareness of fate in all its consequences.

One spends one's life trying to establish independence, to escape the categorizations others wish to impose. No doubt this imposing is part of basic human necessity, and no doubt we all do it, I as much as anyone: put people into classes and assign them to types. And no doubt most people are always trying to escape – except that I think in fact most people, the immense majority, take comfort from being categorized. I too have envied that comfort from afar.

I've lived in the country, yes, but never as an undivided participant. I've worked on farms but never been a farmer. I've observed nature closely but never written as a naturalist. I've been a poet but rarely in the company of other poets. Certainly I have never been a part of any literary group.

The possibility of being *where I am* – wherever, however, whenever – a single eye, an autochthonous imagination, full of sympathy but apart, apart even from myself – is what I always wanted to demonstrate to myself. Where I am is the cosmic individual. Nothing grand, nothing romantic. A duck blown out to sea and still squawking.

APRIL 12TH. MORNING. Gray, overcast, my thermometer just on 32° – fat feathery snowflakes falling, the air filled with them. A few robins run this way and that under the cherry and pear trees in back, looking disconsolate. Do they know disconsolation? Probably not, probably they are aware only of cold, hunger, pain, though I'm never completely sure of this. Is anyone? We cannot know what goes on in the minds of robins.

A couple of weeks ago we had the heaviest snowfall on record in central New York, the Great Blizzard of '93, as it was called by the press, nearly four feet officially. It was exciting. It reminded me of old times. To see snow drifted so high against the windows, immense mounds beyond, expanses of swirled pristine whiteness. Someone has sent me a book about the Great Blizzard of '49, one of many books piled up everywhere here, books I cannot read. When I was a boy I heard repeatedly of the Great Blizzard of '88, in the midst of which my father was born in Sioux Falls, S.D., literally in the midst because no one could come to help and my grandfather was the midwife. No doubt any number of books have been written about that storm. Storms, as opposed to wars, provide the innocent punctuation of history.

After the storm we had thaw and rain, heavy runoff, dangerous floods in the lowlands. Then a few crocuses bloomed in the lawn. And now it is winter again.

My life has been devoted to books – reading them, writing them, writing about them. Here on this bleak hillside I'm surrounded by them. Not a place in this little house is clear of them. I think we should clear a place. Like Deucalion and Pyrrha, Joe-Anne and I should dig into some corner and throw the books behind us until that corner is free, open, clean, until it contains no words, or at least no carefully, laboriously formulated sentences, like these I'm writing here. Maybe the thrown books would turn into something beautiful behind us, like birds. Maybe they would fly away over the valley and disappear.

Beside me on a bookshelf, as I smoke cigarettes and drink coffee, is a bird I am reasonably certain does not feel anything and has no thoughts at all. It is made of solid clay, heavy and hard, about five inches tall from its big clumsy feet to the top of its head. The body is white with crinkles that look as if they were marked in the unfired clay with a toothpick. The face, the thick beak, and the legs and feet are black. I don't know for sure what bird it is, but it looks like drawings I've seen of the great auk, that flightless bird of Iceland whose flesh was so gratifying to the appetites of mariners, men who had fed on tack and salt herring for months, that the species became extinct in the 1840s. This auk stands lumpish and helpless on the bookshelf beside my chair, and I'm not so sure on second thought that it doesn't express something – the sorrow or bewilderment or simple bemusement of the artist who made it. It might as well be the sorrow or bewilderment or simple bemusement of the bird itself, facing extinction. Who the artist was is a mystery; no initials scratched on the bottom to indicate his or her identity and pride of authorship. Yet clearly this is a unique work, not mass produced from a mold; it required time and effort and imagination in the making. I like that anonymity, which at one time, centuries ago, would have been common but is so rare in the ego-culture of today. An oval sticker on the bottom of one foot says: $23. A sign not of the artist but of the entrepreneur. And I suspect the artist was an Inuit from eastern Canada or Greenland, while the entrepreneur was a white invader, still profiting, like the mariners who ate them up, from the hapless auks – to say nothing of the hapless Inuits.

Martha gave me this bird. My daughter, whom I think of so often. She has given similar gifts. On the upper sill of the window across my kitchen is another bird, this one of polished wood with a drooping tail, a crested head, and a face that suggests a tropical species, South American or Asian; a more stylized bird, perhaps a fantasized bird, not identifiable. Under it on the lower sill is a tall narrow ceramic vase that Martha brought from Mexico, tapered toward the top, colored with abstract blue and black designs, now filled with a dried bouquet of pearly everlasting from my friend Isabel Bize's splendid garden. On the bookcase in the next room is a ceramic sculpture of Mexican dancing dogs. On a windowsill in my workroom is a small stone figure of a man in a parka sitting on his heels with his hands on his thighs, leaning backward, slanting a little to one side, looking up with an expression of stoical amusement. He reminds me of men in the drawings of George Price, who is among my favorite artists. Martha brought me this little "Eskimo sculpture" from Alaska. (According to *Webster's International*, the Eskimos, although comprising a single linguistic stock, are divided into sixty-five distinct groups or nations, each with its own name. The name "Eskimo" is not used by any of them.) I like this sculpture and keep it near me all the time. It also has no indication of its maker's identity and the sticker on its bottom says only: 15911 –

anonymity carried to the point of numerical mystery, which is always implicit in it.

Now the snow is falling faster, thicker, the ground under the trees is beginning to turn white, the robins have gone, no doubt to seek shelter in the sumac grove or the thorntrees.

Anonymity of a kind is potential in ordinariness. Her mother Sara and I are the only ones who remember Martha's birth, and now we are in our seventies. Who will remember when we are gone? No one. Knowledge of persons – intimate knowledge, the most meaningful knowledge – passes in and out of existence continually, like persons themselves, in the machine of time. Sara was my first wife, or should I say I was her first husband – or is the fact that we were married at all an irrelevancy now? We separated long ago. But when we were young we were graduate students, neophyte teachers, beginning scholars, writers, and editors, and from 1946 to 1952 we lived in Chicago. Sara's pregnancy was quite normal. When she came to term, however, she was in labor for thirty-six hours and had a difficult time of it. This was at the Lying-In Hospital, as it was called, attached to the University of Chicago Medical Center. And to say that I remember Martha's birth isn't quite right because in those days husbands were certainly extraneous when it came to the birthing itself; we were excluded. Nevertheless I stayed with Sara in the labor room, held her hand, talked to her, talked to the steady stream of doctors, interns, and nurses who came to look at her, though in fact they had little to say to me and treated Sara as if she were a lump of undifferentiated plasma lying there on the cot. From other labor rooms up and down the hall we heard wails and moans, which I think prompted Sara not to utter a peep; she didn't, at least as long as I was with her. Then finally she was wheeled away to the delivery room. I went to a waiting area thinking her pain would be over soon, but the delivery took another four or five hours.

Martha was born on December 6, 1951. She and Sara came home from the hospital about five days later. As it happened that was a time of blizzard. Chicago had been brought nearly to a standstill with all the side streets filled up by snow. I couldn't get my car out. When I called a taxi, none could help me. Finally I located a friend, Ned Rosenheim, and we shoveled out his car and were able to pick up Martha and Sara and bring them home to our rather drab apartment on the South Side. That night Martha cried all night long. She quietened only when I was holding her, walking up and down with her. She was a beautiful baby and I was pained to see her in such distress, so tiny and helpless, and even more I was worried and self-reproachful about my own inadequacy: why couldn't I be of more help to her? Sara, who of course wasn't feeling at all well herself, was worried too. Next afternoon when the pediatrician came to our apartment to examine Martha, which is what they did in those days, we told him about the night before, and he asked: "Did you have the window open?" "We always sleep with the window open," I said. "Well, the baby was cold," he said. I felt like an idiot. After that we kept the window closed and Martha almost never cried.

About three months later Sara decided to move to Alabama, where she had been hired as an assistant professor by Auburn University, and of course she took Martha with her. I couldn't blame her – in many ways I had been in bad shape for a long time and was not much good for anyone – but I was dangerously broken up by their departure. The sense of loss was like an implausible bodily depletion. Later Sara obtained a divorce from a court in Chicago, but by then I had left the city too.

For four years I didn't see Martha. Then Sara brought her to visit me. When they came in the door of the house where I was living, Martha clung to her mother's skirt and pointed at me. "Mama, who is that young man?" she said. She was a beautiful brown-haired, brown-eyed little girl, and of course very southern, lisping in a child's accent from the deep south, at once demure, bashful, and coquettish. Obviously Sara had tried to prepare her for her first cognizant meeting with her father, but Martha hadn't altogether taken it in. How could she? I wasn't exactly on top of the situation myself. I was anxious and doubtful. What does a father say to a daughter who is a stranger?

Well, we became friends quickly. Sara brought Martha to visit a couple of times a year. During that period Martha and I were probably more like niece and uncle than daughter and father, which was natural enough. But we became close. I wrote her many little letters for Sara to read to her, and I wrote stories for her as well. Later, I think when she was eleven, Martha came to see me for the first time on her own, riding the bus from Alabama to Connecticut. When I was eleven I'd never have dared try anything like that. Then her mother remarried, and although Martha's stepfather was – and is – an entirely intelligent, sensitive, amiable guy, the transition to his household left Martha feeling seriously dislocated. Probably dozens or scores of conflicting desires and responsibilities were at work; in this era of broken and reconstructed families we all know what children suffer. Probably she was susceptible most of all to the abrupt new complexity of her life as she was emerging into puberty. To my perhaps hypersensitive noticing she showed signs of an anxiety resembling my own at her age, which she could not perceive, understand, or control any better than I had. This was my first clear intimation that, since I had had no hand at all in her upbringing, emtional illness, or at least the predisposition to it, may be in part transmitted genetically. By this time I was forty and had remarried too; my wife Rose Marie and I had moved with our infant son to northern Vermont. Martha came to visit for longer periods. One summer she stayed at a camp near Ely and one winter she attended a private school near Woodstock. I saw more and more of her. When she was fifteen she spent rather a long time – I don't remember how long – with Rose Marie and me, and when she returned to Alabama she almost immediately became pregnant.

Martha. A young girl bounced around from pillar to post, doubtless getting contrary advice and admonition from everyone, divorced parents, stepparents, grandparents; I even heard at second hand about various teachers and counselors who were involved. I know it was awful because she told me so. She came back to Vermont and enrolled in our local high school, from which in the spring of her sixteenth year she graduated, though she was pretty big toward the end. The school was most cooperative. She was asked to stay at home for the last two or three months, but her lessons were sent to her and arrangements were made for her to take the requisite exams. In the backcountry of northern Appalachia, as some demographers have called Vermont and New Hampshire, adolescent pregnancy was not, after all, unusual. That summer she and the father of her child were married and settled first in our town, then in the next town to the east. And my first grandson was born.

This was one of the happiest times of my life. I was writing well, I had begun to make friends with other writers both in Vermont and elsewhere, I was supporting my family even if minimally and it was a wonderful family. My relationship with my son, who was delighted to be an uncle at the age of nine, was continually joyful to me, I had formed close friendships with my neighbors and was called by name everywhere in town, I was working hard in the woods and fields as well as at my type-writer; in short, I was living a life, which though still confined to a remote sector, could be called almost normal. I was doing what my doctors fifteen years earlier had told me I would never be able to do. And now my daughter and son-in-law and grandson were living nearby. Rose Marie and I were frequent baby-sitters. Martha and her husband were both students at a local college, and they and their friends were in and out of our house at all hours. For the first time in years I was in touch with young people. This was the era of the Beatles, the Stones, "Alice's Restaurant," SNCC and the Weathermen and the Panthers, *Liberation* and Barbara Deming, the whole ferment of the 1960s: the civil-rights movement, the anti-war movement, the imminent feminist movement. My friends, people like Denise Levertov, Mitch Goodman, Adrienne Rich, Galway Kinnell, and many others, were wrapped up in radical politics, and though I couldn't take part in person, except for working with a few local young men who desired to avoid conscription into the imperial army, I could do it vicariously through my friends and through my writing. I did. It was an exciting time, a liberating time, and for me the liberation was personal, meaning more and more freedom from the emotional incapacities that had destroyed the first half of my life, as well as political, a revivification of the radical ideas I had acquired when I myself was a student in high school and college. And all through these years of Martha's adolescence, as we talked our way through her pains and predicaments, her pleasures and successes, I felt closer and closer to her, more and more intensely related to her as one human being to another, and at the same time, imperceptibly and without my knowing it, I became a real father. I don't know when it happened. But by the time she was twenty and I was fifty it was unmistakable.

During the years since then we have experienced many changes in our lives. Martha moved to Arizona, she and her husband divorced, she completed her M.A. in history, she worked as a waitress, social worker, research assistant, a couple of times she was hospitalized for short periods for her anxiety, she remarried, she lived in New Mexico, Oklahoma, and California, she had two more children, she became a painter. She had always been interested in painting, but in her late twenties she began to take it seriously, working on her own, as stubborn and independent about things like that as her old man. She visited me many times in Vermont, we kept in close touch by phone and mail, and I visited her once in Davis, California, where she and her husband lived. He is a paleo-palynologist, a person who works with fossilized pollen to discover not only the nature and distribution of plants in the ancient world but many other things as well, and he was doing research at the university there. I was astonished to see Martha's new work, which was not only imaginative but technically rich and deeply felt, work of genuine maturity. In and around Davis she had discovered many buyers for her paintings and even a couple of collectors. She was a very beautiful woman of thirty-five with many friends, many admirers. I thought she had the world by the tail, so to speak. As for myself, at sixty I moved to upstate New York where I became a professor at Syracuse University, another event that would have confounded my old doctors. My life was busy, not to say frantic – professionally, artistically, sexually, in every way. Probably my friends were saying I was making up for lost time, though that would have been an oversimplification. Eventually I also divorced and remarried. I retired from teaching. I moved from Syracuse to a little house forty miles away among the farms of the Stockbridge valley, and this is where Joe-Anne and I have been living for the past four years.

Already now it is late afternoon. The ground is covered with snow, the air is thick with it. Cars on the highway are creeping by. Through my window – the window from whose sill my little Eskimo friend stares up at me in quizzical and amused reproach – I can see winter in the valley again.

One day when I came home from shopping in Oneida I found the red light gleaming on my answering machine. I spun the tape and replayed the message. It was Martha. She had cancer and she was going to die and could I come immediately?

Martha was crying violently, her voice was shaking, her words were jumbled together and some were unintelligible. It was the most painful message by far I've ever received, yet unbearably eloquent too. No actor on the stage could have been as convincing. Like the famous letter from Bartolomeo Vanzetti, written just before he and his friend Nicola Sacco were electrocuted by Governor Alvin T. Fuller and the state of Massachusetts, this was an artless "work" which perfectly did what art is supposed to do. I called Martha immediately and she was still half-incoherent from shock and fear. Later I replayed the tape, and Joe-Anne and I listened to it together. But then I erased it. I couldn't endure it a third time.

This was on a weekend. The banks were closed and at that time I had no credit card. I borrowed money from Isabel Bize and flew to California the next day, Sunday, and by afternoon was at Martha's home in Davis. She was there, returned from the hospital. She was lying on a big couch or chaise longue, pale, very weak, but calm and even cheerful, as she has been ever since in my presence, with one exception. Like my little Eskimo, she looked at her predicament with irony and detachment, though never with unconcern. The hysteria was gone. I know it didn't pass off by itself, I know Martha struggled against it, I know it was a willed conquest, and I admire my daughter tremendously. She is one of the most remarkable persons I've ever known, and in my line of work remarkable persons are not uncommon.

Friends, I've never seen so many friends, dozens and scores of them: in and out of the house, bringing food, talking, cleaning, taking care of the children, even taking care of me! It was astonishing.

The history of personal illness is a bore to everyone except the person, and often enough to him or her as well. Briefly then, when I arrived Martha had had an uncompleted operation for colon cancer. The surgeon had seen immediately that her cancer had spread to the liver, and on the spot decided her case was hopeless. He closed her up again. This was the point at which I arrived in California. However, further consultation with an oncologist in Sacramento changed the general assessment from hopeless to not quite hopeless, with the result that a second operation was performed to complete the first one. It was awful, but Martha endured it bravely. Then when she felt strong enough she, her husband, and the children moved to Alabama, where Sara could help them and where Martha still had many friends. I returned home to upstate New York.

Since then Martha has been rejected by several high-powered subsidized experimental programs but accepted by a couple of others, she being a "good candidate," young and strong and without other illnesses. Also because she is white, educated, good-looking, and middle-class? Very likely. The politics of all this is appalling. She has undergone major surgeries, including operations to remove part of her liver and part of one lung. She has submitted to several courses of chemotherapy, including a prolonged regimen of chemo administered through a pump implanted in her abdomen. She has been dealt with honestly and friendlily by some doctors, slyly and abominably by others. Throughout it all she has suffered, as have all of us who are close to her, from ignorance and her inability to get straight and comprehensive answers to her questions. She has suffered from terrorizing alternations of hope and despair. (Anyone who has been through it will know what I mean; anyone who hasn't cannot imagine it.) Right now as I am writing this – two and a half years after she was told she had six months or at most a year to live – she is not only still alive but is doing rather well. Except for the regular injection of a saline solution to keep her pump going, except for a few ordinary medications that any of us might take, she is receiving no treatment. She is in pain, she is weak, some days she can do very little; but other days she leads almost a normal life, visiting friends, going shopping, driving her car, looking after her children, etc. She is even painting, though she cannot keep up the strenuous schedule of work that she sustained in former times.

For several months, in other words, she has been experiencing an interlude of respite. I gather this happens rather commonly among certain cancer patients. She has no observable tumors. On the other hand the doctors say that with her history and her type of cancer the mathematical probability is high that presently unobservable tumors exist somewhere within her body. Before long they, the doctors, will resort to further tests and scans. We can only wait.

Waiting is part of all suffering. I don't know if it is the worst part.

What I do know is that the quality of fatherhood and daughterhood which Martha and I have enjoyed is a possible bright spot in the muddle and darkness. I had nothing to do with her upbringing. When she was a child I never had to chide her or tell her to brush her hair or for god's sake to put on a clean blouse before going to school. By the time we began to be close, Martha was in trouble and my job was to be as accommodating as I could, to comfort her, give her refuge, talk with her about cause and effect, choice and constraint, ignorance and awareness. For a while our relationship was, as I've said, more like uncle and niece than father and daughter, and when we came closer to being parent and child our connection had in it no element of hostility or unease – at least as far as I can tell. We were friends first of all, and we still are. Of course I cannot speak about the relationship of Martha to her mother, or about the problems of single parents generally. I know they are very difficult, but they fall outside my experience. Maybe Sara would say that her difficulties as a parent have overbalanced any benefit that has accrued to me. I don't know. We have stayed in touch during the forty years since our separation, but have never discussed any such issues as these. How could they be judged anyway? It would be futile, and I run from it as I have usually run from every judgment all my life. One can only try to report facts. One fact is that although Martha called me in the first emergency of learning about her illness, she chose, I think with good reason, to go to her mother when she decided to leave California. The bond of mother and daughter is profound.

Whatever all this amounts to, I cherish my fatherhood and my relationships with both my children, which are different but equally important. They are among the few truly gratifying rudiments of my life.

Throughout human history the deaths of children have been common. A platitude. When I look back at random in the genealogy of my family, I find, for instance, Joseph Carruth and his wife Sally Allen. Joseph was born in 1764 and died in 1830. He and Sally lived in Northborough, Massachusetts. They had five children, two of whom died before the deaths of Sally and Joseph. One was an unnamed male who lived only a month, the other a female named Delphia who died when she was twenty-two. This proportion, two out of five dead before their parents, seems to be typical, though some couples had many more than five offspring. As I move forward in the genealogy through the nineteenth century and into the early twentieth, the proportion changes a little for the better. But even in our time children die. During the war many, many homes in the town where I lived had gold stars in their parlor windows.

Not many writers have written about the deaths of their own children, though there are exceptions – John Engels and David Ray come to my mind immediately. It is too difficult. The most famous elegies for children, like Ben Jonson's epitaph for the unidentified "Elizabeth, L. H." or John Crowe Ransom's "Bells for John Whiteside's Daughter," have been written about other people's children. My attempts to write poems for Martha have failed. Of course Martha is still living, and now I have some expectation, as I didn't for quite a while, that she will outlive me. But in a sense I have been – as she has been, as everyone in our family has been – close to her death for a long time. And close to her life too, the re-examined, revalued, precious life. It has been a continuing experience. Days, weeks, months, and now a couple of years spent in fear and grieving. In anguish too extreme to be expressed. I cannot say how I have felt because literally there are no words for it. Of course there are no words for the experience in any poem before the poem is written, which is why poetry is an art. But with certain extreme experiences, not only are words inadequate but the whole language in all its potentiality is inadequate. We are deprived of language, deprived of speech; we are animals, howling.

All our vexation over the relationship between art and life, the imagination and reality, comes down to this: art and the imagination can never be adequate. Art in its nature, as I've said elsewhere, is always a mitigation. The act of writing about reality, painting it, even photographing it, changes it and hence inevitably destroys it. We say we rely on poetry to "transform" reality (as if it could do anything else) or to give us the "meaning" of reality, but if we've transformed it or imagined a meaning in it we've destroyed it. And no documentary, as we call them, can ever be realistic enough to escape art. I know that in one sense a poem or other work of art is continuous with reality, a phenomenal object like a brick or a hibiscus or anything. But to the extent that they "express" reality they are apart from it. Only hysterical messages like Martha's on my answering machine – and I use the term without any of its disparaging connotations; we all know hysteria in our own minds at least occasionally – can come close to reality, and they are hysterical precisely because they fail. They absolutely cannot succeed. Nothing in an interposed medium can be the thing itself. Our lives in art, whether we make it or respond to it, are centered precisely on dumb futility, the way being is centered on nothingness. We who make art must know this and must inform those who are the responders. We must do it repeatedly. Otherwise art is all sham and mendacity, and neither truth nor beauty can come from it.

What do we do in our lives? We resort, weeping and shrugging, to the acknowledged sham of convention, of formulaic utterance. May Martha live long. Please.

After several more surgeries and other extreme interventions, Martha died on November 17, 1997.

TED PATCH'S SISTER, whose name I unfortunately can't remember (and who was also "Dry Dryden's" sister), lived with Ted all her life, was his housekeeper, and never set foot out of his house. When you went there to look for Ted, she would open the door, stand sidewise in it, look resolutely at the doorframe, and say, "He ain't here."

"Do you know where he is?"

"Nuh."

"Do you know when he'll be back?"

"Nuh."

"Well, thanks anyway."

She'd shut the door. She never looked face on at anyone, maybe not even Ted. No one ever told her she was sick. "Funny," they called her.

I wish no one had ever told me.

FIGURING BACK, I'D SAY it must have been 1929 when pupils in the third grade at Mitchell Grammar School in Woodbury, Conn., were given the Stanford-Binet IQ test. Connecticut was said at the time to have one of the best public-school systems in the country, paid for with funds still accruing from the sale of the Western Reserve in the early eighteenth century; this is what we were taught at any rate. The Stanford-Binet test, long since discredited for its bias toward middle-class Anglo literacy, was then still new and well-regarded. What the state expected to achieve by administering it to all its third-grade pupils I don't know and can scarcely imagine – except that it couldn't have been done in our properly egalitarian school systems today. But I believe the state was trying to do its best. Mitchell Grammar School was the least of schools, but still the teachers, all of whom I remember, were well-trained, certified, devoted, convinced of the importance of their work. They took the test seriously.

I scored high, well up in the classification of genius. It was a disaster. From the first grade on my teachers hadn't known what to do with me, in part because my father had taught me to read and write when I was four years old. I always already knew what I was supposed to learn. They put me at the back of the room in a corner by myself and gave me books to read. In those days, even though Connecticut was a wealthy state and the educational system was reputed to be "advanced" – hence the intelligence tests – we still had four teachers and four classrooms for the eight grades of grammar school, a small step up from the one-room school of the previous century, so that the third grade, for instance, occupied one half of a room and the fourth grade the other. When a girl or boy in the fourth-grade half didn't know the answer to a question, the teacher would call on me, and from my place off in a corner of the lower grade I'd give the answer. Not for long, however. I learned soon enough that my ostracism was only made worse by this, and I began saying, "I don't know," which probably never fooled anybody then or since though it became and has remained my standard answer to every question. Some readers of my reviews and essays, including some of my editors, have complained about it.

The teachers wanted me to skip a grade, or maybe two. But my parents, who were conscientious and trying to be up-to-date, wouldn't permit it. They had read in a book by some predecessor of Dr. Spock that children should be kept in their own age groups, that skipping ahead in school would lead to disadjustments. Maybe that was right. I don't know. I labored – the right word, even though the academic side of the program was easy for me – through eight grades at Mitchell Grammar School and never found a solution to that problem.

As for me, what I wanted and wanted desperately was to get rid of my specialness and bury myself in commonness. I did my best to ingratiate myself with my classmates outside of school and to some extent succeeded; I had close friends in those years. I made myself a good, but not the best, marksman with a slingshot. I made myself a good, but not the best, player at marbles, both ring taw and pooning. I became a fast skater and took my part in prisoner's base and other games we played on the ice. At the swimming hole under the iron bridge on the West Side I became a fair swimmer and a courageous, not to say reckless, diver. And so on. I spoke in the accents of my friends, the girls and boys from the farms, listening to them, imitating them. Beginning at age six or seven I dissociated myself as much as I possibly could – not enough – from my family. I never spoke with my friends about what I read in books, though at home in the attic I continued to read a good deal, and I certainly never spoke with them about the fears and uncertainties that engaged my thoughts.

Many years afterward, when I was in my late sixties, I spent a couple of weeks in a mental hospital in Syracuse, and there I was subjected to "psychological testing" that lasted two days. Most of the tests were intended to discover and expose this or that aspect of my personality, but a couple were measures of intelligence, and again, according to the report I was shown, I scored very high. In a way this was gratifying because in the intervening years I had been through all kinds of hell – alcoholism, electroshock, very long periods of treatment with narcotic, hypnotic, and psychotropic medications – and although my memory had been damaged, apparently my crude mental capacities had not. I remember saying to the psychiatrist in charge of my case that what I'd been searching for all my life was a woman who was smarter than I was, so that I could quit all the masquerade. She said: "Not a chance." I was confirmed in my experience, which was not so gratifying. To become a psychiatrist, for instance, she had been through a course of study that appalled me – pre-med training, med school, internships, I don't know what all – a course of study to which I would never think of submitting myself, yet I was clearly smarter than she was, as she readily acknowledged. And she was a tough no-nonsense woman who had achieved her place in life against the odds and had suffered hardships – the ones I knew about – along the way. The people I've known personally whose intelligence, which I can only define as quickness and acuteness of understanding, was superior to mine can be counted on the fingers of one hand. It would be foolish to do that, of course. But I don't mind saying that the one who dazzled me the most – I'm speaking of those I've known personally, not of artists and scholars whom I've met only through their works – was Paul Goodman. Yet I've *felt* inferior to almost everyone all my life.

No doubt the consequence is obvious to people who have read my poetry. My early experience among my schoolmates in rural New England may not have been the only reason why I've written so often in languages not my own, but it is a substantial reason. Nor is it the only reason for my life in isolation later on, away from the world of glitzy literary brilliance in Boston and New York, the world I've glimpsed through my friends, Denise Levertov, James Laughlin, Adrienne Rich, Galway Kinnell, and others, for that matter the world I often enough have wanted and in which I've even known that if I could only find an entry I might shine there as well as anyone. But at a tender age I was taught to fear myself and the least promotion of myself, and this has lasted all my life. It has been reinforced over and over again. I've fought

against it and in recent years, in my sixties and seventies, have some-
what, though never wholly, prevailed. But in my middle years much of
my best poetry – poems like "Marvin McCabe," "Regarding Chain-
saws," "Eternity Blues," the asphalt georgics, etc. – was written in this
fear and hence in common or colloquial speech. Some was in archaic or
poetic speech, or in the characteristic speech of particular intellectual or
professional sectors. Literary conventions, the guises of history, were
important to me. Almost always and in hundreds of different ways I
have submerged my ego in camouflage, fronts, deceptions of all kinds.
Call it obfuscation but I hope not obscurantism. Usually I have been un-
aware of it. It has seemed the natural thing to do.

Well, I hope the work is honest fundamentally.

But is it? I don't know.

A FURTHER NOTE: not in grammar school, not in high school, but at
some time later I came by gradual stages to see that my "I don't know"
was more than mere evasion. I knew many things, I had a "photo-
graphic memory," but in issues of substance, including moral issues, I
truly didn't know. And neither did anyone else, at least that was – and
is – my understanding. Knowledge is a function of ego, and like ego ex-
ists in the concrete world; it has its importance. But to transcend ego, to
become an authentic subjectivity, to become undetermined, was what
life in its fullest potentiality was all about. Knowledge was arrogant and
condescending, as I knew for years and years and then found ever more
indubitably when I became an academic: the university is full of the
empty bluster of the cognoscenti.

The ancients were right: what one seeks is wisdom. But they were
also a little naive, having never suffered the degradations of mass culture
and technocracy. The greater part of wisdom is its inaccessibility. Yet I
still believe in the efficacy of straight thought – when it is in the service
of magnanimity.

> *Some was fiddlin'*
> *Some was diddlin'*
> *Some was fuckin' on the floor,*

I was in the corner
Like little Jack Horner
Puttin' the blocks to the Winnipeg Whore.

That was one stanza, the only stanza I remember, of a long bawdy song which Martin's uncle from Arizona used to sing at our parties every summer when he and his wife came east in their Winnebago for a visit. Martin's uncle had done well – I don't know whether in farming or something else – and had retired to the southwest. His song pretty well reflected the tone of social life in our neighborhood in northern Vermont twenty or thirty years ago. We'd be sitting around on the front stoop or at the picnic table, eight or ten of us, with beer and vodka, chicken and ham and corn and potato salad and pickles, on a warm summer night. The dogs would be down in the brook worrying a turtle or off chasing rabbits. The kids would be in the back yard doing god knows what.

Martin himself did not know how to speak to a woman except in sexual – and inevitably sexist – terms. "Hey Rose," he'd say to my wife, "how's your pussy today?" Or, "Why'nt you meet me out in the woodshed later on? Carruthie won't mind." To Rose Marie, born in Middle Europe and raised in the mode of German baroque sentimentalism, this was unspeakably vulgar, and she did her best to avoid Martin, which wasn't always easy. Martin and Midge lived only twenty rods or so down the road. Theirs was the only house we could see from ours. Rose Marie used to think I was out of my mind when I told her that her aversion to Martin's ways was depriving her of a true friend and that Martin was one of the sweetest guys who ever walked the earth, one of the most generous and helpful.

It was a clear, head-on conflict of cultures. To my mind neither Rose Marie nor Martin could be blamed in the least for their manners and attitudes with which they had been imbued, without their knowing it, from earliest childhood. For Rose Marie, for instance, though sexuality was banned as a topic for casual rapping, scatology was not, and a fart – a poopsie – was always a source of jocularity. And Rose Marie was also the salt of the earth, and still is.

Midge or Midgie – short for Midget; her real name is Frances – was not as small as her name suggests, but I reckon she must have been the smallest child in her family. She was maybe 5'3" and weighed 100 pounds. A pretty woman, an appealing woman, with black hair, dark eyes, a smiling face, a good body. Smart as a whip.

FOR YEARS I HAVE wanted to write about the Parkhursts and have schemed to put them into one of my "Vermont poems." But I could never think of a way to reduce them to the dimensions of a poem. The idea offends me anyhow. I'll see what I can do in prose, though I'm not confident of the outcome.

What bugs me is the number of times I use the word *though*. This is more than a verbal tic, it's a deeply ingrained ambivalence, a radical uncertainty – never being able to say one thing without also saying its opposite.

When my wife and I first moved to Vermont, Midgie was nineteen and pregnant with her fourth child. Rose Marie and Midgie became friends quickly, which was owing to Midgie's intelligence and openness, because we were an outré couple in that essentially Appalachian society – a beardy poet and his wife who spoke with a foreign accent – and could easily have been spurned from the beginning, as indeed we were in some sectors. But Midgie knew better. She used to come to our house frequently, sit at our kitchen table with one child in her lap, another clinging to her knee, the third running helter-skelter. But she controlled them and took no nonsense from them. Rose Marie took Midgie aside and talked to her about birth control. The people of the backcountry in those days knew about condoms, of course, but were too impatient to use them or too poor to buy them; more sophisticated methods of contraception were unknown to them. Rose Marie's advice worked, and after her fourth was born Midgie had no more children.

She was lucky. We knew women who had ten or a dozen kids, all of them huddled together, often, in a little trailer in the woods with a leaky roof and not much in the icebox.

Ten years later Midgie and Martin decided it would be a good idea for Martin to have a vasectomy. I was surprised when Martin agreed to this, it was such a departure from the sexist norm of that society – surprised and pleased. "Carruthie, I'm gonna get my balls cut off," Martin announced. He went down to a hospital in Williamstown, I think, where the deed was done. Afterward we were sitting around in their living room, five or six of us, and I said to Martin: "What'll you do the next time Midgie gets pregnant?" Instantly his arm flew out straight at me. "I'm gonna shoot you!" he said.

One time we were sitting around the Parkhursts' kitchen and Farnum Emery from a mile up the road toward Waterville was there. Farnum said: "You know how to tell a good cat? You pick him up by the tail and if he don't holler he's OK." Just then the Parkhursts' old tom came wandering in, raggedy-eared and bleary-eyed, and Farnum reached down and jerked him up by his tail and held him out at arm's length. Tom was so astonished he didn't utter a peep but just hung there. "By God," said Farnum, "that's one hell of a good cat!" And he dropped him back onto the floor.

MARTIN QUIT SCHOOL in the sixth grade and went to work. Book-learning was not for him, but work was. He enjoyed work, he believed in it. When I first met him he was holding down two jobs, driving the grain truck for the Lamoille Feed Company in Morrisville during the daytime, dressing off birds at the chicken factory in Wolcott at night. He has continued driving the grain truck to this day, distributing grain to farmers from seven in the morning until two or three in the afternoon. In the old days feed was handled in hundredweight sacks, which Martin spent all day heaving around. He is tremendously strong. More recently the grain is kept loose and is fed into the truck, then into the farmers' storage bins, by blowers, which eliminates the lifting and carrying. A boon to grain-truck drivers, you might say. But since the change Martin has suffered seriously from back trouble, which has crippled him from time to time and kept him off work for extended periods. Maybe he'd be better off if he'd had to continue rousting the grain sacks by hand.

Martin is not illiterate but I think close to it. I never saw him read a newspaper, for instance. Midgie does all his paperwork, keeps his accounts, even writes checks for him, and she acts as his "front man" in other ways too. If you call Martin on the phone Midgie always answers, and even though Martin is in the same room the conversation is conducted through her; you hear Martin telling her what to say and then you hear her saying it. A certain redundancy. I remember one time I was doing my income taxes and I didn't have enough money to write a check for what I owed. I called up and explained my predicament to Midgie. She relayed it to Martin and I heard him say, "Tell the son of a bitch there'll be a check laying on the kitchen table in the morning." Then Midgie said, "Martin says there'll be a check on the kitchen table in the morning." Sure enough, when I went over next morning the house was empty, the door was, as always, unlocked, and the check for $500, which was a lot in those days, was on the kitchen table, signed by Frances Parkhurst.

For years Midgie has worked out. She's been housekeeper to several affluent families around town. At the time of my tax problem her three older kids were in school and she took the youngest with her when she went to work.

Make no mistake, Martin came from the bottom end of the social scale in our region. Not from the lowest rank, which is reserved for the ne'er-do-wells who for one reason or another, often paranoia, can't hold a job and who live in broken-down shacks – the backcountry has plenty of these – but from the next-to-the-lowest. His family were never farmers; they couldn't afford to be. They were laborers, working out for other farmers or working on the road crew for the county. Sometimes they drove trucks for the talc mill, sometimes in the old days they were gandy dancers on the St. Johnsbury and Lake Champlain Railway. Midgie's background was about the same, although I believe she completed high school.

Like many people from the underclass Martin is profoundly intimidated. He takes no interest in politics and never attends town meeting because he feels instinctively that such matters should be left to his "betters." His social and political ideas are maxims received in childhood and often enough deformed by prejudice. When I first went to Vermont I overheard the kids at play calling each other "nigger," even though they had never seen a colored person in their lives, and when the older folk talked about big business or government at all they always blamed "the Jews" for everything that was wrong, even though at that time no Jew had ever set foot in the town or the county or, for all I know, the state.

Once after I had moved away from Vermont I went back on a visit and took my girlfriend with me, a good-looking woman whose features were easily recognizable as Semitic by people in the city. We were in the old house – Crow's Mark – when Claude Lahouiller stopped in for a drink. After a bit Claude said to Judith, "What you be? Irish?" She laughed and so did I. As Claude was leaving he pointed to me and said, "Watch out for 'Aydie. He got all his brains in his pecker." We laughed again and Judith gave me a look.

Midgie and Martin own their house and have owned it ever since I've known them. They've improved it in many ways. They have a barn and a toolshed and a pleasant yard with big maple trees and a lawn and flowers that Midgie has planted. In the back is Martin's vegetable garden, which he tends assiduously, and in the fall they work together to harvest the crop and make it ready for the freezer. Martin and Claude always used to wager on who could produce the first edible peas. In April Martin would be out in his garden, planting, when snow still lay in the hollows and the frost wasn't hardly half out of the ground, and sometimes he'd lose his peas and lose his wager. But sometimes the peas would survive and Martin would sock the expensive fertilizer – 20-20-20 – to them, and he'd have a delicious crop before the middle of June, which was a wonder.

Martin was a hard worker and a hard trader. As the years passed he became more and more engrossed in trading, and he had the ideal job for it, driving his grain truck out among the farmers every day. He'd see one farmer who wanted a pickup, for instance, or a good springing heifer, and another perhaps twenty miles away in the opposite direction who had a pickup or a heifer he wanted to get rid of. Martin would buy and sell and make a profit. Not always – once he bought an old Fiat from me for $100 and discovered three days later that it couldn't be fixed and had to go to the junkyard – but usually. The truth is that by the time he was forty Martin had plenty of money, though this didn't change him or Midgie or their way of life an iota. And in the matter of the broken-down car, he refused to take back his $100 when I offered it to him. That was typical of him, typical of backcountry Yankee probity in general. It was okay to skin somebody but not enough to hurt him, at least not badly, and if you got skinned yourself you didn't complain.

Once Martin and I were talking about one of his fellow workers at the feed mill who was dying of cancer and making a fuss about it. "What's the good of complainin'?" Martin said. "When it's time to go you shut up and go."

ONE TIME, PROBABLY in the late sixties, I was working at night in my cowshed where I normally stayed all night for quiet and a refuge from other chores. Often when I quit at about six I'd take my mail out to the mailbox by the road just as Martin was driving by in the grain truck on his way to work. He'd stop, roll down his window, and holler (he never spoke in a moderate voice): "Carruthie, how the hell are ya this mornin'?" On this particular night, however, someone banged on my plank door at about two o'clock. It startled me. I was used to absolute quiet and privacy at that hour except for the animals around me in the woods. I opened the door and Martin was there, leaning somewhat unsteadily against the side of the shed.

It was late winter. Snow was falling, a wet and greasy snow. The road was treacherous – "slicker than owl shit," as we used to say. Martin had spun out on the corner above my place and run off the road into a good-sized stump beside the brook. He'd been drinking. "My own goddamn fault," he said. "I was slidin' it, showin' off to myself on that goddamn bend up there." Then he added: "We got to get that fuckin' car outa there, Carruthie."

Martin was always scared of losing his license, on which his job depended. He had a few marks against him already with the troopers and the warden.

We walked down the road and woke up old Phil Stearns (whom I called Stan in my poem about the chainsaw). Phil wasn't happy about being routed from bed at two in the morning, but he came anyway, bleary-eyed and raspy, and cranked up his battered old Powerwagon, which had a winch on the front of it. We drove to where Martin's car was. The front end of the car was stove in, the grille smashed, the radiator still steaming, the headlights bent out of line, but otherwise it looked all right, certainly mendable. We hooked up the winch-cable, snaggled the car out of the trees, onto the road, and towed it to Martin's place.

"Here," Martin said to Phil. He held out a twenty.

"Get off my fuckin' back," Phil said. He stomped off into the snow.

Martin had hit the steering wheel hard when the car made impact with the stump. He had a bad pain in the region of his sternum. "Damn fool," Midgie said. "Get yourself in my car right now, we'll go to the emergency." But Martin refused.

"You fetch me to the hospital," he said, "you know they're gonna tell the troopers."

I urged him to seek help too, but he still refused. "Maybe you did something to your heart," I said, though I didn't really think so.

"Fuck it," he said.

A few days later he did go to Doc French over in Hyde Park and had himself x-rayed. He'd broken some ribs and cartilage, very painful but not dangerous. In a couple of weeks he was okay.

But the morning after Martin slid off the road I looked for that busted car behind his house and saw it was clean gone. I never could find out what he did with it. Maybe towed it with the grain truck to some remote swamp up toward Eden Mills and abandoned it, or took it to some farmer's place, or maybe to Dave's junkyard over toward Elmore. Whatever he did he didn't do it legally, I was certain of that. No recorded transfer of ownership and registration. That car just vanished. Nothing left but my memory of it. It was a dark green, four-door Dodge sedan, which was the kind of car Martin favored.

"Carruthie, you keep your trap shut, right?"

Which I've done – until now.

ROSE MARIE, WHO HAD been chased out of school when she was a child by the Russian army, was working on her GED, then became a student at the university in Burlington and eventually completed her M.A. She worked hard, and I worked hard too, taking care of our son, hacking in my cowshed – reviewing, editing, ghostwriting – to earn enough to pay the school bills. Now I think of this as one of the principal accomplishments of my life. But the point is that like country working people everywhere we became extraordinarily busy. I recall thinking sometimes what a pity this was. We had no time to enjoy our place in the world. In the fall, for instance, we were surrounded by the justly famous autumnal foliage of northern New England – looking out from Clay Hill across the valley toward the Sterling Range during the first week in October could truly take your breath away, it was such a brilliance and prodigality of color, which hundreds of thousands of tourists traveled hundreds of thousands of miles to see – and yet we could scarcely look at it. That was the time when, in addition to our regular work, we were harvesting the garden: beets, carrots, beans, broccoli, leaf vegetables, corn, tomatoes, squash, turnips, parsnips, potatoes, apples; gathering them, transporting them, cutting them, cooking them if necessary, putting them in containers, storing them in the freezer or in their bins and boxes in the cellar – and often enough I had deadlines hanging over me at the same time and was pounding the typewriter until I couldn't think straight. We hardly noticed the colors of autumn, and then before we knew it the season was over.

In their own ways Midgie and Martin were as busy as we were, as busy as everyone was who was making it in the backcountry in those days.

Nevertheless Midgie was in our house frequently and the kids were in and out continually. Martin was the one who never came. Once in a while during the summer he'd walk over and sit with me on a maple block next to the woodpile or inspect whatever project I was engaged in, building or tearing down, digging or leveling. One time I had the motor of a car spread all over my lawn, and he just stood for a moment in the midst of it and shook his head and walked home again without a word. But he never came in our house. In this he was like most of our other neighbors on the hill, especially the men.

But once he broke his rule. Midgie had hepatitis and was in the hospital in Morrisville, badly ailing. It was a question whether or not she could survive. At the worst of it Martin stumbled into our kitchen one night without knocking and stood there, crying and blubbering. "What am I gonna do?" he said. "What am I gonna do?" He couldn't say anything else. I don't know what we said or did, probably the usual insufficient things, "Take it easy, Midgie will be all right, etc., etc." – useless. I think maybe we offered to look after the children, which would have helped a little. But Martin was on his own, cut off, like anyone in such circumstances, and after a while he went away.

He was completely dependent on Midgie, not just for help with practical matters but in every way. Yet he was an unspeakable domestic tyrant at times, especially when he was drinking, and abused both Midgie and the children badly. From our place we could hear him roaring and bellowing in the night.

The other time I saw Martin cry was when one of the children, I think John, was badly injured in a snowmobile mishap. The boy was ten or eleven years old and of course shouldn't have been driving a snowmobile at all, though most country boys did. His feet had gotten jammed down between the tread and the frame somehow, and he was in danger of losing them altogether. Somehow the boy crawled home, and when I got there Martin was holding him in his arms. Tears were streaming down his cheeks. Midgie was the collected one, as usual, and she brought the car, opened the door, and drove them off to emergency in a hurry. The boy's feet were saved.

TWO OR THREE TIMES I drove to Morrisville behind Midgie when she didn't know I was there. A trip of ten miles. She drove with a passion, sixty-five, seventy-five miles an hour on a small road, whisking that big Dodge around the turns and around other cars as if it were a kite in the wind. She was totally competent though she looked about fifteen years old behind the wheel. When she became a grandmother at thirty-five she still looked no more than twenty. I became a grandparent myself at forty-eight, which I thought was decidedly premature, but when I complained about it to the neighbors they only hooted at me.

WE WERE GAMBLERS in those days. Poker was our passion, or one of them. Think of it not as the glitzy recreation of the uppercrust but as the enormous subculture of the poor, thousands and thousands of poker games every night in logging camps, farm kitchens, roach-infested apartments of graduate students and ghetto menials. Why anyone would go to Vegas or Atlantic City to play the house's slots or blackjack or keno, thus enriching those who obviously need no enriching, when there's a friendly poker game around every corner and all you pay to play is the price of a little beer or coffee, is more than I can understand.

We'd gather after supper, usually once a week, in the Parkhursts' kitchen.

Martin and I, Farnum, Claude and Paul Lahouiller, two or three others. Fifty cents for the kitty and a dollar limit. Small-time. Yet the pots often reached a hundred dollars and more. The betting was fierce and the Frenchmen were crazy anyway. They were the ones who always wanted, at the end of the night, to play double or nothing, to "go for broke" as they said in their bitten-off accents. "'Aydie, whatsa matter wit you, you got no balls?" But Martin and I were more prudent, if only a little, and refused that folly.

The Lahouillers had come down from Québec a couple of decades earlier, the father and mother, who were remarkably successful immigrants, and five sons. Jean, the oldest, had become a carpenter and then

a contractor and then a developer, a successful businessman who sel-
dom played poker. Camille, called the Manager, ran the home farm in
the valley; he played occasionally. Claude had another farm a little to the
west, and he was a regular, as was Paul, who had no farm at that time
and earned his living in ways not altogether obvious. The youngest,
Denis, pronounced Denny, was still in school, was into drugs and drop-
ping out. He stayed away. At times he would disappear for days or
weeks. At times it seemed as if the whole Catholic puritanical and aspi-
rant weight of the family rested on Denny.

Claude had been the first person I met when I came to northern Ver-
mont. He was only nineteen then. When I took my first walk up the
road I found him mowing the lawn at the place of a wealthy woman, a
summer person, on top of the hill. We talked for twenty minutes and I
think I understood at least one word in every ten that Claude said to me.
It was bewildering. But I soon found that I couldn't understand the
Anglo inhabitants any better than I could understand the French. They
both spoke a strange dialect, which I learned after a while.

When I was dealing I usually proposed five-card stud, a rudimentary
game in which one's luck is quickly determined. But the others, espe-
cially the Frenchmen, liked high-low, a seven-card game with four up
and three down, aces either high or low, in which both the best and the
worst hands were winners. More often than you'd think, one player
would have both. Not infrequently two or three players would have
both – or would think they had – which would produce the kind of ex-
citement the Frenchmen loved and the rest of us loved too but were
somewhat scared of. The betting would be furious and prolonged. The
showdown would be desperate. But the cards are immutable and
adamant; somebody would have a five-card flush in spades, ace high, for
the best hand and also ace, two, three, four, six in mixed suits for the
worst, and he would rake in the winnings, an armful of fives, tens, and
twenties, with triumphant hoots and cackles. And we'd all have another
taste of whatever we were drinking.

At the end of the night we'd lean back in our chairs and laugh. A hell
of a time, we'd say. Then we'd go out to the cars and take off in the dark
one after another. Martin always had four or five cars and trucks in front
of his house and when visitors came the number could be twice that
and more.

Sometimes I was too broke to play – I never had as much money as the others – and then I'd just watch or go into the parlor and talk with the wives, Midgie, Patti, Diane, Deb, and the others. Their talk was more interesting than their husbands'. They'd be drinking beer and eating chips, yet they were all slim and good-looking – I don't know how they did it. Diane was a dark-haired, dark-skinned beauty who had a cast in one eye – exotropia – so that you couldn't tell where she was looking, and somehow this made her more attractive and sexier than ever. Midgie would make coffee for me because I didn't drink alcohol at that time and didn't care for coke, and I'd drink enough coffee to wire me as tight as an egg-slicer, and then I'd walk home. Sometimes I'd keep on walking, I'd go up into the woods and sit under the spruces until I was calm enough to sleep. Or I'd sit by the brook in starlight and let the water-music run in my head until a poem came.

ONCE CLAUDE'S BARN burned down. Half the town turned out to build him a new one and three days after the fire Claude was back in business. Luckily it was in summer and the cows were out when the fire started. A month later Claude and Patti had a pig roast. The pig revolved all day over the maplewood fire on a spit turned by a bicycle chain on a big sprocket attached to an electric motor. An iron cauldron hung from a tripod over another fire nearby, filled with boiling salted water in which the ears of corn, hundreds and hundreds of them, were cooked in their shucks – the best corn I've ever eaten, after I burnt my fingers getting the shucks off. Some of the men had a corn-eating contest, and Luther Parkhurst, Martin's father, ate forty-eight ears. I could scarcely believe it. Of course that was spread over an afternoon and an evening, with plenty of beer for lubrication. I felt a little out of it at that pig roast, a little alien. Still everyone was good to me, and I've never forgotten it. When the pig was finally done, they slung it onto a trestle and Luther carved it for all the pig-eaters. It was delicious.

All the first sons in the Parkhurst family down to Martin were named Martin Luther and were called by one name or the other alternately to tell them apart.

MARTIN AND I SHARED a spring. A "water right" was written into my deed. The spring was in back of the Parkhursts' house under a bank that sloped down from one of Marshall's hayfields. In winter Marshall would spread manure on that field, and every spring when the runoff began Martin would call me up, the only times he himself ever spoke to me on the phone. "Carruthie," he'd say, "there's cowshit in the water."

"I believe you're right," I'd say.

"What're we gonna do about it?" he'd say.

"I'm fucked if I know," I'd say.

Then Martin would emit one of his characteristic growls – arrrgh – and hang up.

There really wasn't much we could do. Eventually at our request Marshall quit spreading manure on the lower part of that field, but the runoff from the upper part, and for that matter from half of Butternut Mountain, still flowed down into our spring. It was a fact of life that the old-timers accepted. They would have scoffed at some, though not all, of our ideas of "purity" today. Hell, they'd have said, a trace of cowshit in the water never hurt anybody. And since many of them worked in cow barns and half the time were covered with the stuff, maybe they knew what they were talking about.

The spring box was wooden and old and half-rotten. We were losing a good deal of water. So one time we decided to improve the spring, and we hired Gerald Tatro to dig it out and install a couple of big concrete tiles, the lower one perforated, the upper solid. Then he packed the lower side of the spring with clay. It worked. It also cost $495. Martin and I were standing there after the work was done, admiring our new contraption.

"I'll match ya for it," Martin said.

We got out our lucky half-dollars, flipped them in the air, caught them, slapped them against the backs of our hands, keeping them covered – an ancient ritual I've never seen described in print (so far is literature from the real affairs of life). Then, since Martin had offered to match me, I was the one to uncover first. Heads. Martin slowly lifted the edge of his hand and peeked in.

"Shit," he said.

I'd won. Martin had to pay the whole bill. It was damned lucky for me because I'd have had a hard time coming up with the four ninety-five. But of course I didn't let on to Martin.

"You better get yourself a new half-dollar," I said.

"Arrrgh," said Martin.

In fact over the years, however, I think we came out about even.

That spring was a good one, had been known for generations as reliable and a source of good-tasting water. In earlier times it had served another family too, but that house had burned down, and a one-room schoolhouse as well, located up the hill a little way from the Parkhursts. The schoolhouse had been abandoned, and once I tried to buy it for an office. It would have been ideal – spacious and well-lighted. Marshall, who owned the land, was willing to sell, but the town, which still owned the building, couldn't give me a quitclaim deed without extraordinary red tape, so the deal fell through. In the old days our neighborhood, the area serviced by the school, had been a distinct settlement three miles from town, which was a not inconsiderable distance when you were traveling on foot or by horse. I used to think of this often and with a certain gratifying sense of kinship when I was whipping downtown in one of my old junkers to buy a nine-sixteenths coarse-threaded nut at the hardware store for three cents. From old-timers who are now all under the ground, up in the Plot Cemetery, I heard about life in those earlier days. They had dances on Saturday nights in the schoolhouse, eight or ten families together, and also readings and recitations and games. It must have been a good life, even though a hard one as it was. Especially in winter when the snow lay five or six feet deep everywhere. They used to "roll the roads," i.e., pack down the snow solid with a huge roller filled with water and drawn by a four-horse team, and then they put special shoes on the horses with sharp cleats so the animals wouldn't fall on the icy surface.

Farther up the road on my land, next to the woods, was another spring, even better. The best water in town, everyone said. It had a wooden trough that carried the water to the roadside where it spilled into a barrel, and this was where the horses stopped to rest on the hard pull up the mountain. The previous owner of my place had been paid two dollars a year to maintain the watering barrel. When I was there, of course the horses were gone and no one paid me anything. But I kept a dipper hanging on a tree for anyone who wanted a drink.

Down in the village was the Cold Spring, fitted up with stone and concrete, benches and steps. Many people used it. When our spring ran low, as it did sometimes in dry summers, we took our containers downtown to get water for drinking and cooking. For bathing we used the brook.

The qualities of life in the old settlement persisted after the old ways were gone. I never had better neighbors anywhere than Midge and Martin. Or Marshall, the Jennisons, Sadie and Phil Stearns, Ray Latourneau, or any of the others. We shared. We helped. We made one another laugh even when the hardships were greatest. And we were all aware that we lived in one of the most beautiful places in the world, which in many ways, mostly indirect, enriched and stabilized our lives. I'd be there yet if anyone in Vermont had given me a job when I needed it. Instead I've been in exile for thirteen years in upstate New York, a meaner region. I don't care for it. Am I bitter? One isn't supposed to admit such a thing in polite society, but of course I am.

IN MATTERS OF LANGUAGE I've always been a stickler for detail. I suppose I've been a conservative. We see more and more, as for instance in ecological matters or in education, that the radical position *is* conservative, a desire to conserve and retain values that the merely liberal mind is willing to throw out for the sake of reform. But how often this desire is misinterpreted!

When I was teaching I tried to induce among my students a functional understanding of the distinction between *lay* and *lie*, or between *who* and *whom*. I tried to show them the advantage of learning grammar and using a dictionary. But many of even the most intelligent writers in my graduate workshops, and for that matter many of my colleagues on the teaching staff, could not take it in. Why? they would say. What's the difference?

When I told them that love and devotion are the root of it they merely looked askance.

You choose correctly between *street car*, *street-car*, and *streetcar* not because the choice makes a substantive difference – it doesn't – but because you care for language, you are in love with it. A good carpenter cleans and puts away his tools properly, so does a good gardener or a good cook, and no one will ever convince me that a worker who ignores his tools will do satisfactory work. Appearances may be and usually are deceiving, especially in the arts, but Allen Ginsberg cares as much for language, and uses it with as much deliberate concern, as did Elizabeth Bishop or Robert Lowell.

If you are male your attitude toward language is analogous to your love of women, and vice versa. A lover does not mutilate his or her beloved, except in cases of insanity.

Logic is of not much value in itself, but an attention to logical analysis, such as lexicographers strive for in determining the historical meanings and stylistic attributes of words, denotes a respect for the human mind and hence for humanity in general, and this is what has been vanishing in my lifetime. My students could not see this. Human beings have a capacity for thinking as well as a capacity for suffering, and the two are closely connected if not combined, but my students responded only to suffering, not to thought. They could not see that if they shut out the one they will soon shut out the other and end in indifference. Frankly, this appalls me.

When I earned my living as a literary hack I did a good deal of copyediting for publishers in New York, including my friend James Laughlin of New Directions. Jas, as I call him, and I agreed. Yet certainly no one could accuse James Laughlin, the principal avant-garde publisher in this country for fifty years or more, of literary conservatism. Attention to correct historical judgment, we felt, means respect for one's work, one's associates, and oneself. I looked up everything in *Webster's New International Dictionary*, the second unabridged edition, and I even bought a copy of it, a new one, for thirty-five dollars, which was more than I could readily afford in those days. It still rests on a table in my workroom and is used many times every day. Believe me – or believe any copyeditor – you need to look things up, you cannot rely on guessing or memory. *Phys-ics* is hyphenated one way and *phy-sique* another. *Knowl-edge* is hyphenated after the "l," not before it. If you know enough about language you can figure these out for yourself, but it will take time and effort. The lexicographers have already done it for you. Relying on lexicographers doesn't result in decorum in the usual sense, or in stiffness or inhibition or pedantry. Many authors, probably most, who have been published by New Directions have used colloquial speech in their writing, slang, intentional and literal outrageousness of all kinds. They have used bizarre punctuation and divergent spelling. They have tried everything that love of language can suggest. But they have never been neglectful – never. Carelessness was always the mark of a bad writer. Yet to me the common American mode in poetry today seems based exactly on a kind of strange, premeditated, literal carelessness.

When I was writing my asphalt georgics I used a good many hyphenated words not only to keep the syllabic count, which I could have done without hyphenations anyway, but in order to find unusual rhymes. This wasn't merely expediency, however. It was care. I looked up every hyphenation to make sure it was correct before I let it into the poem. Jas also in his poems has used a lot of hyphenations in making his lines conform to the typewriter prosody he invented years ago, and he looks them up to be sure they're right. Maybe I got the idea from him, I don't remember. But I've admired his poems for a long time and have written a few of my own in his manner. I like that kind of writing. An arbitrary, artificial structure makes composition easier for me; not harder, as most people think. It gives the work greater force and fluency. You can't build a house, no matter how inventive or fanciful it may be, without a sturdy frame.

I learned more about language – structure and mechanics – from studying Latin in high school than I ever learned elsewhere. I loved Latin and I was good at it. Unfortunately, in my senior year I was the only student who wanted to continue and the rules wouldn't permit a class for one student; that was the end of my formal education in classics. Then in the army a few years later I was chosen – a great stroke of luck – to be trained as a cryptographer, what the army called a code-and-cipher clerk, though in the field we used only ciphers, never codes. I enjoyed that training also as much as any I ever had, and in three months learned as much as I've ever learned in so short a time. Even now, fifty years later, I break the cryptograms in the newspaper every day, though I long ago gave up crossword puzzles, anagrams, and other word games, including that supreme idleness called Scrabble, as a waste of time. When I was a graduate student at the University of Chicago, my favorite courses, taught by Professor Hulbert, were in early English, and to this day one of my favorite books is Otto Jespersen's *Growth and Structure of the English Language*. Does this fascination with words, grammar, the mechanics of language make me inevitably a fussbudget and a pedant? Has it hurt my poetry? I don't think so. Writing sonnets can make a poet foolishly punctilious and academic, as we have all seen in numerous instances. But writing sonnets can also liberate a poet's natural gift for lyricism and his or her deepest, most authentic, determining emotions. It depends on the poet.

MY LIFE IN MUSIC began, as far as I remember, when I was three years old, shortly after we moved from Waterbury to Woodbury. I was sitting on the linoleum-covered floor of the central room upstairs, which we called "the hall," in front of our old Victrola. My mother put on a record of "The March of the Tin Soldiers." The music was remote and tinny. I can still hear that strange timbre, as if the sound were coming from another world (as in a way it was). I was enthralled. My mother played the record over and over for me. Before long I learned how to climb on a stool and crank up the Victrola myself, and put on the record and listen to it with my feet bouncing and my whole body straining and dancing. I probably haven't heard that tune in more than sixty years, but I can still sing it effortlessly.

The record was a thick, heavy disk with one side blank and a red label. The Victrola stood on a matching walnut cabinet that held a few other records, mostly operatic, Schumann-Heink and Caruso. I played these other records too, but they didn't appeal to me as much as the instrumental music, the band music, and this has been the case, with a few exceptions, ever since. The Victrola used wooden "needles," three-sided pegs about half the thickness of a pencil and an inch or so in length, which you sharpened in a tool that resembled a pair of pliers or a paper punch; you inserted the peg and squeezed the handles, and the end of the peg was shaved off on a bias, so that one of the three edges became the point. I loved to do this, or to work with any tool, and I used up a good many needles when my mother wasn't watching.

(Once in Waterbury when I was about one and a half my mother found me in the kitchen standing on top of the gas range with a burner turned on, flicking sparks from the flint-and-steel gadget that was used to light gas stoves in the days before pilot lights.)

Of course I must have heard music earlier than this. For some reason I can't remember my mother singing to me then or later, and it's possible she didn't. I remember only her whistling, which she did well and constantly as she went about her household chores. On the other hand I do remember my father's singing because it was so awful. He couldn't carry a tune to save his life; he couldn't even come close, and his singing was a mournful monodic hooting that moved me only to a sense of affliction. But it was his job to put me to bed at night, to read to me and sing the nursery rhymes, as he did bravely and miserably. My mother was just the opposite. She had nothing to do with my bedtime, but she had perfect pitch, which I was lucky enough to inherit.

A couple of years later we bought our first radio, an Atwater-Kent with a speaker that stood on top. This was my mother's greatest joy. From that time until she died forty-five years later she listened to the opera every Saturday afternoon, and to every other program of serious music she could find. Undoubtedly this was in part what turned me off to most classical music from an early age, but especially opera. The shrieking sopranos and bellowing baritones of the 1920s and 1930s seemed to me anything but musical, and I was fascinated by music. (Drama meant nothing to me, then or now.) I played everything I could get my hands on: Jew's harp, bones, spoons, jug, kazoo, ocarina, harmonica, pennywhistle, ukulele, guitar – but unfortunately not the piano, because we didn't have one. If I couldn't find anything else I'd stretch a rubber band between my fingers and the bedpost, and play on that. Making musical sounds was my obsession.

For me the best was the pennywhistle or tin whistle: technically, an upright six-hole fife or flageolet. I used to buy them not for a penny but a dime at Woolworth's in Waterbury whenever I got the chance. They were made from stamped tin with a wooden fipple, painted gaudily on the outside; flimsy things that quickly bent and rusted. Nevertheless I became a virtuoso. I quickly learned how to sound the accidentals, i.e., sharps and flats, and to play in five basic keys, two up and two down from the "open" key (which was usually c). Of course I couldn't, at that time, read a note and had no structural understanding, yet I could play almost anything I heard, including operatic bits from my mother's radio. To this day the tin whistle (now made of chrome steel with a plastic mouthpiece) is "my" instrument. From age six or seven to beyond seventy it has been, when I come to think of it, the most constant factor in my life.

Of course in those days everyone sang and children most of all, in school, at play, around campfires, wherever. We sang sentimental songs like "Juanita," and "Jeanie with the Light Brown Hair," Civil War songs like "Tenting Tonight" and "The Battle Hymn of the Republic," railroad songs like "She'll Be Comin' round the Mountain" and "I've Been

Working on the Railroad," spirituals like "Swing Low, Sweet Chariot," black folk-songs like "Old Black Joe," and hundreds and hundreds of others, including many hymns and carols. Also songs of the subculture, such as endless pornographic verses to the air of the "Toreador's Song" from *Carmen*. All this was outside the home and apart from the home. Home was *Tannhäuser*, the *Fifth Symphony*, and concerti by Liszt, Tchaikovsky, Franck, etc., a place where music and the idea of music were held in reverence and one was a listener, not a participant.

Nevertheless I began to take violin lessons when I was twelve, and I progressed quickly. My teacher thought I was a prodigy, as in a way I was. She pushed me hard. After a year I was playing Paganini caprices – but badly. Even then the curse of neurotic repression and alarm was upon me and I couldn't loosen up enough to play well. On the violin when I tried to make a proper vibrato the whole fiddle would shake and chatter under my chin so that I could never produce a really good tone, and sometimes I would misplay a passage simply because my fingers were clamped so tight to the strings. In school I broke pens continually because I gripped them so hard and bore down so heavily. I couldn't help it. Even now the plastic barrels of ballpoint pens fracture in my hands.

Through high school I continued playing the fiddle, took lessons from a fifty-cents-an-hour near-charlatan who was all we could afford, and sat in the second-violin sections of a couple of orchestras, but when I went to college I left the instrument behind. I haven't touched it since.

I was a set-up for jazz. Talented but unable to play, also unable for whatever reasons to participate much in the music respected at home, yet at the same time acutely craving musical expression, my own or any-one else's, I needed jazz, needed it desperately, long before I really knew what it was. It was forbidden of course. I didn't have to ask. For my parents jazz was not something new and exciting but something already degenerate, the acculturation of whorehouses and speakeasies. In this they were close in feeling to the great majority of intelligent, literate people of their time. It was not a question of race. Our home admitted no bigotry, at least not of that kind. My parents must have known that jazz came from the south and had been originated by African Ameri-cans, but as good radicals they would have said it was not an art but a mere social phenomenon, a symptom of exploitation and declassi-fication, like ungrammatical speech or drunkenness. For me it was – or it became – the appealing social antithesis of what I knew, what I was expected to know, and consequently it fascinated me. But beyond that, in intonation, texture, rhythm, and all its sensuous qualities, jazz moved me viscerally from the beginning. The slurred notes and off-the-beat phrasings made me respond autonomically inside as if I were an animal in a mating dance.

As I've said many, many times it was music, real music. It was spontaneous, heartfelt music. Apart from all the social and other adjuncts fastened to it in the public mind, it was complexly organized sound – vibrations moving through the air.

For years I've thought the first jazz record I heard was Benny Goodman's *Stompin' at the Savoy*, but that wasn't issued until 1936 and clearly I've been mistaken. Either what I heard was Chick Webb's original version of the tune by Edgar Sampson, or perhaps some other number by the early Goodman band – the one with Bunny Berigan and Bud Freeman in it – which over the years became conflated in my memory with *Savoy*. Or I may have heard something else altogether. It doesn't matter. What I know is that it was brought home from private school by our town's only rich kid, and it made an impression on me which I do remember – the event more than its content. It was immensely important. But at the same time I was buried in a small agricultural town in New England, as remote from jazz then as Siberia is today – though in fact I imagine people in Irkutsk and Yakutsk can hear plenty of jazz if they want it – and nothing much happened in my relationship to jazz – I still didn't know what it really was – until after my family moved to Westchester County, New York, in 1935.

Then I began to hear more and more jazz. I've written about this elsewhere, no need to reconstruct the details here. In high school and college my interests went in two directions, toward the black swing bands and their remarkable sidemen, the bands of Ellington, Basie, Lunceford, Kirk, Hopkins, all of them deriving from work done in the 1920s by Fletcher Henderson and Benny Moten, and on the other hand toward the music of New Orleans and Chicago, the small freely swinging groups playing essentially unarranged numbers from a standard repertoire. But in those days we didn't think a great division separated these styles. Sidemen from the big bands often played in small groups working in the mode of ensemble improvisation, and true musicians from New Orleans and Chicago, people like Zutty Singleton, the De Paris brothers, Darnell Howard, Albert Nicholas, Davey Tough,

Jimmy McPartland, even Bix Beiderbecke, often worked in the big bands. Not until after the war, after the bop revolution, did deeper divisions among musicians of different ages and from different regions, working in different modes, become conspicuous. And when it happened I regretted it. I even resented it.

In high school and college I met others who were interested in jazz, but not many. We were still in those days thinly scattered in most of the country. White people who listened seriously to jazz were oddballs, rather disreputable oddballs. We formed a kind of avant-garde, and even in those days, though I knew little about literature of the twentieth century, I thought an affinity ought to exist between admirers of jazz and readers of *Ulysses* and *Lady Chatterley's Lover*. It didn't. Serious writers before the war had no interest in jazz as music but only as a degenerate social and cultural phenomenon which could be evoked in writing sometimes sympathetically and sentimentally, as in the work of Joseph Hergesheimer, but more often disparagingly, as in T. S. Eliot's *The Waste Land*. I believe jazz was not accepted in white American literature on its own terms until the 1950s and even then by only a few percipient independents like J. F. Powers and Kenneth Rexroth.

However, a few of the jazz people I met in college were both more knowledgeable and better off than I. They could teach me. They had records and record players. This was extremely important. I didn't have a record player of my own until 1946. At that same time jazz was becoming available on radio, and at home and later in my dorm room I had a little AM set that could bring in remote broadcasts from hotels and ballrooms late at night, segments of Earl Hines from Chicago or Erskine Hawkins from the Savoy Ballroom in New York. I listened with the sound turned way down and my ear up close to the speaker. Moreover at least a little jazz, and sometimes a lot, was mixed into the copious productions of the best white swing bands of the period, Goodman, Herman, Shaw, Barnet, etc., and could be heard on jukeboxes everywhere. When I had a chance to invest a nickel in Tommy Dorsey's "Marie," for instance, I would do it gladly and would put up with the stupid arrangement – Dorsey's smarmy trombone and Jack Leonard's bland vocal against the unison singing of silly responses by the whole band behind him – for the sake of the solo by Bunny Berigan, which still seems to me one of the great trumpet improvisations of all time. Lovers of jazz then and earlier always have had to search for it wherever they could find it, often enough fixed within the effusions of commercial dance bands like an exquisite brooch on a frilly bosom.

During this period and beyond, the tin whistle remained my chief means of making music for myself. I learned to play things like the Berigan solo in "Marie" and other famous pieces, but mostly I jammed by myself or with the radio, and later, records. When I was able to buy a whistle tuned to B-flat, this became easier. Then in about 1949 or 1950, when I was living in Chicago, my friend Andy Park (Robert A. Park) loaned me a clarinet and offered to teach me to play it. Of course I accepted. This clarinet was the older kind with the Albert system of fingering, which was favored by most of the early reed players from New Orleans. I was delighted with it. I found that my facility with the tin whistle helped a good deal in learning; after all the six-hole pipe was the prototype of all woodwinds. I began improvising on the clarinet almost immediately, developing a bluesy tone, experimenting with slurs and glisses. I loved it. I was working in a publishing office at the time, burdened with too many duties, taking home a heavy briefcase every night, but I made time to practice. Andy helped me to relearn the reading techniques I hadn't used since I quit the violin and apply them to the clarinet. He also helped with things like the slap-tongued staccato and how to play high notes clearly and with proper intonation. Once a week or so we would play simple duets based on transcriptions of themes by Mozart and Beethoven. Occasionally I played with Don Ewell, the jazz pianist who was my good friend at that time, doing things like "Grandpa's Spells," "Someday Sweetheart," "Wolverine Blues," "Sugarfoot Stomp," etc., simple tunes that were part of the standard jazz repertoire and that I knew well.

But I left Chicago and moved to New York not long after this. I gave Andy back his clarinet. For a while I didn't have one, which was disturbing. Then one afternoon when I'd been drinking in a bar on Third Avenue, I said to myself, "What the hell," and walked up to Schirmer's on 43rd or 44th Street, and bought a Paris Selmer for $750, which was an enormous amount of money. I paid for it on the installment plan and never regretted it. A Paris Selmer was not quite top of the line, but close to it, a beautiful instrument. I was living on East 32nd Street in a big one-room flat. I bought Mozart's *Clarinet Concerto in A* and taught it to myself, not caring that I was playing it on a B-flat instrument, and for reasons I didn't and don't understand the neighbors never complained. When I entered the psychiatric hospital in 1953, I worked with the musical therapist there on the Mozart and on other pieces, which helped a lot; it was the first time I'd had a trained musician to play the piano accompaniments. He was an organist, a member of the Guild, working in the hospital to earn extra money, and I wish I could remember his name. A few times I played in front of his organ accompaniment in the empty hospital auditorium, our sound echoing in the big chamber – it was a great experience.

In 1955 I left the hospital and entered a period of nearly total seclusion that lasted five years and of somewhat less than total seclusion continuing another ten or fifteen years beyond. During the first part of this, I had time on my hands. I played the clarinet four or five hours every day. Though I still played jazz and blues, I concentrated more and more on European music, striving for purity of tone and clarity of phrasing. I still have the scores I used then, which I ordered from Schirmer's: many transcriptions from Bach, Mozart, Haydn, Beethoven, Chopin, Paganini, etc. Also an adaptation of Mendelssohn's *Violin Concerto*, clarinet music from Von Weber, Brahms, Debussy, Schumann's *Fantasy Pieces*; such things as Hindemith's *Sonate* from 1939, Milhaud's *Concerto* from 1942, Copland's *Concerto* of 1950, Artie Shaw's *Concerto for Clarinet*, Alban Berg's *Fäntasiestucke*. Of course I had to play these without accompaniment and often I had never heard them. It was difficult. Hence my discovery of Music-Minus-One Records was a momentous event. These were recordings of clarinet ensemble music with the clarinet part left out, so that the musician at home could play with the record, filling in his or her part and thus participating in a full performance. It wasn't like playing with live musicians, of course, there was no give and take; yet the other parts were well and imaginatively done, and I learned a great deal. I remember Music-Minus-One recordings of the Mozart *Quintet* and *Concerto*, some early wind sextets and octets by Beethoven, and other pieces. But the one I liked best, the one that helped me the most, was Brahms's *Quintet*, which I still regard as one of the finest pieces of music ever composed – complex, original, even daring, yet deeply felt and expressive – I still listen to it from time to time on my CD player. I worked on that piece for a couple of years. And at the point when I had mastered it I think it's safe to say I was a pretty fair amateur clarinetist, even though I had never played in an orchestra or a live ensemble of any kind.

Incidentally, I should say that in high school and college I heard live jazz whenever I could scrape together the means to do so, and in Chicago I heard it often and regularly at the Bee Hive on 55th; Jazz, Ltd. on the Near North; the hotels downtown; joints around 63rd and Cottage Grove or out on Western Ave. But after I left Chicago I heard no live music for many, many years. I was totally dependent on records and the radio. Even now I rarely go to clubs or concerts because, although I can do it if I have to, I still don't really enjoy myself in public meeting-places.

During those years of seclusion I also played the tenor recorder, working on duets with my friend Tom Appel, who lived next door and was the only person outside my family I saw for five years. I enjoyed this, but more for the company than the music. Later I played a few times in recorder quartets and quintets, which met at the house of Tom's friends in Chappaqua, but I was too nervous to play well in a group. The fact is I never really cared for the recorder. Next to the clarinet it seemed plummy and fat.

After I moved to Vermont I continued to play the clarinet when I could, and at one point I taught myself the rudiments of classical guitar, but music more and more had to take a back seat to my work in the fields and woods, the garden, the barn, and of course to the heavy schedule of hacking in my cowshed. I quickly lost my embouchure. A time came when I didn't play the clarinet for more than an hour a week, then an hour a month. When my son took trumpet lessons I played duets with him and taught him the "Tin Roof Blues," etc., but this was only for about a year.

As time passed I lost more than my embouchure. From childhood I had been short-winded, a genetic narrowing of the air passages that makes it difficult to exhale completely. By the time I was forty this had been made much worse by smoking. I had to struggle to play the longer phrasings without losing my breath altogether. And then more recently I've been troubled by another problem, which I've never investigated – just an additional revolting intimation of impending collapse, I say with a shrug – but which is probably caused by a hardening of the soft palate in old age. I can no longer retain wind pressure in my head after I've played for half an hour or so: the air escapes through my nose in little burps like steam escaping from the pressure cap of an overheated radiator. How absurd!

Yet it doesn't greatly matter. Although I'm still regularly seized by a desire to blow when I hear other musicians blasting away on some good medium-tempo blues like "c-Jam" or "After You've Gone," I no longer feel really deprived, as I did so desperately, disconsolately, at one time. Often I've said I'd rather be a musician than a poet. It's true. The affective responses to poetry and jazz are not the same, obviously, but to the extent that they can be compared, jazz has meant more to me than poetry. I know, I've known all my life, that I could never be a musician in the public sense, and I've suspected, much of the time though not always, that even if my failings of personality were removed at one stroke by the Impossible, I'd still be no better than a middling musician. Well, I'd have been satisfied with that, I'd have been delighted and overjoyed by that (leaving aside for the moment what everyone knows about the hardships of a musician's life). What could have been better than being a musician and working every day in a free and genuinely creative fashion at a time when jazz was the newest, the fastest developing, and by far the most expressive style of imaginative interaction with reality. I believe jazz has been both a consonant accessory to and an eloquent articulation of every serious artistic, social, cultural, and philosophical happening in my lifetime. I wasn't able to participate, except by writing about it and by letting music influence the rhythms and sonorities of my poems. But that's okay. Now I'm just glad I was alive to hear it.

MIFF MOLE WAS A GREAT trombone player. Gunther Schuller calls him an "extraordinary musician" and a "pioneer trombonist," who in the early 1920s, when jazz, especially white jazz, was truly in its infancy and struggling to break away from the mold of the ODJB, "set standards of playing for years to come." I'd say myself that the standards were never really lived up to until J. J. Johnson came along. Mole did what Teagarden, Harrison, and Lawrence Brown never did, assimilated the New Orleans concept to trombone virtuosity and jazz inventiveness. He played in the manner of collective improvisation, using the traditional call-and-response patterns, submerging himself in the collective concept, yet at the same time brought new ideas to his work and was as inspired a soloist as anyone. What he lacked was Teagarden's ability to charm, or perhaps just Teagarden's desire to be charming. He was anything but a cut-and-dried tailgate trombonist, far better, for instance, than Georg Brunis or Jimmy Archey. For a few years, mostly around 1926–28, Mole and Red Nichols, working together under their various noms de musique, produced astonishingly good jazz.

But by 1950 Mole was long past his best years. He was playing at the Bee Hive on 55th Street on Chicago's South Side in a revivalist band that also included Don Ewell, Darnell Howard, sometimes Muggsy Spanier or Punch Miller. Mole played what was required. He was OK. In his solos he spent a lot of time messing around in the pedal register, making grunts and groans, with occasionally an upward leap into treble brilliance that showed something of his old flair – but not enough.

I used to see him on the street in Hyde Park sometimes in the afternoons. I believe he lived somewhere around 53rd and the lake. He was a man of average appearance in every way: gray hair, medium build, dressed in suits that needed pressing, wearing a bow tie and a fedora, a little seedy but a little jaunty too, as if he were half-heartedly pushing himself to keep up a former sharpness. He would be standing on a corner, looking around. Doing nothing. Alone. A quizzical look on his face, as if he were saying to himself, "What the hell am I supposed to do now?" I have no idea what became of him after I left Chicago, except that he died in 1961. He was born in 1898.

The old age of jazz musicians has always seemed especially troubling to me. Leaving aside the fact that many of them have become "old" at a time of life when most people would still be considered middle-aged or even young, only a very few – almost none – can do good work for more than a few years. A few who become so popular that they remain in demand can continue to work, to enjoy a good living, even when they are playing poorly, and we all know examples of this. Most just fade out and disappear. They become bartenders or small-town music teachers or god knows what. I always think of Joe Thomas from the Lunceford band, a splendid musician, who vanished and then came to the surface again working in an undertaker's parlor in Kansas City. Imagine the quality of his old age. It must have been truly pitiful.

The emotional intensity required of jazz musicians cannot be sustained. If drugs and booze and constant lack of sunshine don't do them in, then the forces of inertia will. They lose concentration, they begin to repeat themselves, they become careless and hit too many clinkers. This is not the case with some other musicians. Horowitz could go on playing with intensity when he was in his seventies and eighties, he could bring passive emotional fervor to the materials he was not creating, his performances were acts of appreciation and love, which, as long as one's fingers haven't become arthritic, remain possible for classical musicians in old age. But a jazz trumpet-player cannot really sustain himself by replaying his old solos, or even the solos of Louis Armstrong or Bix Beiderbecke or Dizzy Gillespie. Jazz is not constituted that way. The context is all wrong.

Deliberate composers and arrangers can do it. Ellington remained active all his life. His art was reflective. Even so it can be argued that his last compositions are unfocused and reveal a lack of imaginative control compared with his best earlier work.

If a case can be made for pensioning artists early – and obviously it can – then jazz musicians deserve first consideration.

YESTERDAY WAS THE FOURTH of July. Here in upstate New York, and I presume in most of the rest of the country, newspapers, radio, and TV have been full of admonitions against the private use of fireworks. It is illegal here anyway, but for the past two weeks or more, my neighbors' kids have been shooting off firecrackers and twirling sparklers as usual – or actually more modestly than in the past perhaps, judging by the amount of noise. It hasn't bothered us. It becomes harder to obtain fireworks, even illegally, as the years go by. When I think how it used to be when I was a kid, back in the 1920s, what people have now is nothing.

In those days fireworks were cheap, plentiful, and in no way prohibited, either in law or in the general notion of propriety. The Fourth of July was a serious holiday and was seriously celebrated by capitalists and socialists alike in every town and village from coast to coast. Parades, speeches, and all the rest of it. And fireworks – the rowdiness and vulgarity of fireworks, which had been a conspicuous part of the celebrations from as far back as anyone could remember. Farther, in fact. Fireworks were an important element in the social cement that held society together, something everyone accepted, something beyond the purview of individual taste or standards of conduct, like the Mardi Gras in New Orleans. My parents were prissy and anxious when it came to child-rearing, but even so I was permitted to save up my money for months beforehand in order to buy firecrackers, and I think, though

I can't remember for sure, I was actually given money to supplement my savings.

We had Chinese crackers, two-inchers, cherry bombs, six-inch salutes, ribbons of caps for our cap pistols, torpedoes (which exploded when you threw them against a hard surface), snakes (nuggets of slow-burning powder that spouted coils of gray, snake-like ash when set afire), and others I don't recall. Older boys had blanks they fired off in their fathers' revolvers. *Bang, bang, bang, bang, bang* – all day our village sounded like a frontier settlement in the transports of self-destruction. Haven't our capitalists always made sure that gunpowder is abundant, economical, and accessible? And on the Fourth who could fault them?

Yes, all these things were dangerous. In my memory the worst were the ordinary two-inch crackers, which had enough powder in them to make a very satisfactory explosion but were cheaply manufactured. For fuses they had merely twists of gray paper that had been saturated with low-grade powder. Some burned fast, some slow, some almost instan-taneously. We were warned never to hold them in our hands when we lit them, but of course we knew better, since part of the pleasure of fire-crackers is throwing them at something or somebody. We had narrow escapes. No one came out of the Fourth of July without minor burns and contusions. But the only serious injury I remember was when my friend Jay Richards accidentally shot his younger brother, who was called Deedee, in the face with a blank .22. Somehow the boy's vision, blacked out for a while, was okay the next day; but as long as I knew him he had powder burns on his forehead and specks of powder buried in the skin of his nose and cheeks.

Naturally we experimented. We set off six-inchers inside coffee cans and blew them sky-high. We threw ignited cherry bombs in the river or buried them under sand. We tossed two-inchers at passing cars to scare the bejesus out of their drivers, who of course were ready for it and had their windows rolled up or their side-curtains in place, no matter how hot the day, and hence weren't scared at all. We stuffed strings of Chi-nese crackers into holes so they'd all go off at once. We made cannons out of iron pipes and stuffed them with firecrackers and pebbles and blasted away at streetlamps and legions of Nehi bottles.

The Fourth was not just for children, however. Mr. Fray, our neigh-bor across the road, had a real miniature cannon with wheels and a breechlock, which he set up in his dooryard and fired at noontime, using – I think, but I'm fuzzy about this and my home research hasn't helped – a form of carbonite that can be detonated by adding water. At any rate it made a fine percussion. "Do it again, do it again!" we kids would always shout. But Mr. Fray knew that the mystery and charm would be ruined by too many manifestations. One shot was enough.

Parents in fact came into their own only after dark. Mr. Fray and my father would combine forces to buy a stock of skyrockets, Roman candles, St. Catherine wheels, fizzers and sparklers, which they brought home in brown paper bags – sources of much excitement and anticipation. After supper the Frays and Carruths would set up chairs in the Frays' field next to the barn, and all of us – a dozen or so – would gather, the women with shawls to shield themselves from mosquitoes. The older boys, Bobby and Croft, stood by with shovels to put out grass fires if any started, but I don't remember that any did. Mr. Fray and my father would then set up the fireworks one by one and discharge them. Puny little things, I know now. The skyrockets went maybe twenty or twenty-five feet in the air and produced nothing but a stream of sparks. The St. Catherine wheels spun for half a minute, sputtering and smoking. But we were enthralled. It was one of the truly big events of the year. I got more pleasure, I'm sure, from those little displays than from any of the grander municipal and commercial shows I've seen since then, though at the same time I really do love all fireworks, the big exhibitions with their noise and splendor, and I go to them whenever I can. Maybe fireworks are the best combination of artistry and technology; I wouldn't be surprised. Once I read an account of an annual competition in Tokyo. All the principal Japanese manufacturers bring their most spectacular devices and set them off over the bay for everyone to see and judge. I'd give a good deal to be there. And all my feeling about fireworks comes, I believe, from those little family celebrations more than sixty years ago.

After they were over we would eat watermelon and the men would smoke. To this day the smell of burnt powder and tobacco and the taste of watermelon go together in my mind. Then we'd disperse to our houses.

Looking back, I see another element of those celebrations which was known to me at the time though I couldn't have said what it really meant. The Fourth of July was the one time in the year when my father participated in any communal activity whatsoever, the one time he even spoke (except for good-morning and good-evening) with a neighbor. For all I know he may have hated it and feared it. If so, he kept this to himself, as he kept almost everything. But because of this brief connection between my father and Mr. Fray I think the Fourth was the only time when I felt genuinely at ease in my little spot on the interface, as we say now, between my family and the world. When the Depression came, the good times – if the term can apply to something so trivial that happened only once a year – ended. The Carruths and the Frays could no longer afford fireworks. Then the Carruths moved away. Never again did I experience anything resembling this easy interaction between my family and the community. It never existed.

I WAS NAMED AFTER my grandfather, or rather after two-thirds of him. His name was Fred Hayden Carruth, and he was called Fred by his family and friends. But at some point, I don't know when, he decided that his *nom de plume* would be simply Hayden Carruth, and he may have done this when he was still in his teens and freelancing for the papers in Minneapolis. He had been born in 1860 in Lake City, Minnesota, a town on the Mississippi where the river widens extraordinarily, making in effect (though not in fact) a lake, like the Tappan Zee on the Hudson River near Tarrytown where my grandfather later lived. Lake City was – and is – an attractive location. When his mother died, leaving her husband, my great-grandfather Oliver, with five or six kids, the old man remarried quickly, choosing a widow, Sarah, who also had five or six kids and – what was more important – a prosperous gristmill of which Oliver became the manager. And the whole family, kit and caboodle, lived together in a big house attached to the mill. In the course of time – not long – my grandfather married his stepsister Ettie. Thus we have a family joke about incest in our ancestry: our grandfather married his sister. Not true, of course, and the joke gets rather tiresome.

What has always fascinated me is what went on in that house *before* my grandmother and grandfather married. All those young people jammed together, both sexes, various ages but mostly adolescents. I have visions of delightful orgies. I know my grandfather was a somewhat raffish person all his life. On the other hand my grandmother, years later when I knew her, was a hardshell prairie Baptist who probably did nothing improper her whole life. And I know that her first child, my uncle Oliver, was born at a decent interval after the marriage.

It must have been a common arrangement in those days after all, large numbers of stepchildren living together as their parents struggled to make a life for themselves in adverse circumstances. But the vision of orgies persists and is a source of charming gratification in my mind.

My grandfather took his bride westward to the town of Estelline in the Dakota Territory, where he and a partner, who was a printer, established the first newspaper in that region. There is no need to recount his history; it resembles that of thousands of other men and women who have migrated from the west to New York City, where they have become moderately successful as artists, writers, theatrical people, etc. My grandfather went to work for the *Tribune*, later for *Harper's Weekly*. He freelanced for other publications. He published a number of books. In the 1920s, when I knew him, he had ended up as the fiction editor of a popular women's magazine, where he remained until his death in 1932. For a number of years, from the 1890s until World War I, he was a minor but accepted personage in the literary community. He wore spats and a lavender waistcoat, carried a silver-headed cane, belonged to the Players' Club, and had his portrait drawn by James Montgomery Flagg, the famous illustrator who did the recruiting poster during World War I; he knew such people as Stephen Crane, John Kendrick Bangs, and scores of others in the writing game, as it was called, including such poets as Joaquin Miller, Lizette Woodworth Reese, Bliss Carman, and he had at least a passing acquaintance with the greats, Twain, Howells, London. At the same time he never lived in the city, but always somewhere out of town – Pocantico, Poughkeepsie, places like that – and he was a good family man who fathered six children, two of whom died before reaching adulthood.

When I was born my father wished to name me after his father, for whom he had enormous respect, but my mother said she refused to have a son named Fred. She was quite clear about that. She prevailed – one of the few times she did – and I was named simply Hayden Carruth, with no middle name.

I was perhaps eight or nine when, one afternoon on my way home from school, I was in a small general store on Main Street in Woodbury trying to decide what to spend my weekly nickel on. Behind me I heard someone say my name. It came out of the ambient undertone with remarkable clarity, like a clarion. I turned quickly. No one was looking at me. A woman I didn't recognize was at the dry-goods counter talking to the storekeeper with her back turned toward me. I was startled and puzzled, but then I understood: she was talking about my grandfather, how much she enjoyed his writing. She had no idea who I was. Astonished and sobered, I left the store without buying any candy.

That was my first inkling of what a literary reputation in one's own time might be.

IN THE 1920S MY grandmother and grandfather lived in a small house they had built, first as a summer place and then as a year-round residence, on Hardscrabble Road in Briarcliff Manor. Now this is a posh suburban enclave with winding drives and pretty houses, but when I first knew it it was still farming country, although a few well-to-do families had established themselves there. One of my chores when I visited my grandparents was to walk up the road every day and fill a half-gallon aluminum can with milk at a neighboring dairy barn. In back of my grandfather's place was a good-sized hill, partly open, partly wooded, from the top of which on a clear day one could see the Woolworth building in Manhattan thirty miles away. It was called Flag Hill, though I no longer remember why. One of my clearest perceptions of my grandfather, because I saw it many times, is of a man in his sixties with a fringe of longish white hair striding through the tall unmown grass on Flag Hill with a big walking stick in his hand and an Irish setter, named Danny, bounding at his side. Often only Danny's head would be visible, and then only when he leapt to see over the top of the grass. I used to wonder if my grandfather was writing something in his head when he went walking.

When he was in his cabin I knew he was writing. The cabin was a one-room building in back of the house, about fifty yards away, covered with gray asphalt shingles to match the house, and in fact it looked like a little house with a peaked roof, a doorstep, windows on all sides, yew and juniper growing against the outside wall. Inside were bookshelves, cabinets, a worktable, a typewriter, lamps, letter scales, paper cutters, all kinds of fascinating paraphernalia, including a stand-up desk at which my grandfather did most of his work, using India ink and an old-fashioned penholder with a broad steel nib. His handwriting was spectacularly bold and beautiful, but illegible. For years I tried to imitate it, without much success. In fact everything about the cabin and my grandfather's work was an enchantment for me. Long before I had any understanding of what he really did, i.e., when I was only two or three years old, I knew he was the most colorful and attractive person in my little world. And he himself did everything he could to foster my admiration. I was his first grandchild and his namesake. On my first Christmas he gave me a copy of his most popular book, *Track's End*, bound in stiff boards and blue leather with gold stamping on the cover, inscribed to "my first grandson" in his distinctive hand, and this remains today the oldest personal possession I have.

One of my grandfather's stories was about Horace Greeley, the famous publisher and editor of the *Tribune* in the days before my grandfather joined the staff there. Greeley had terrible handwriting. Only one typesetter in the composing room, an old man who had come to the paper with Greeley, could read it. He was famous for it. He set all Greeley's editorials. One day the younger men in the composing room decided to play a trick on the old man. They got a hen, inked her feet, made her walk back and forth over a piece of copypaper, then gave the paper to the copyboy to spike on the old man's hook. When the old man arrived at work, he came to his typecase, sat on his stool, grabbed up the paper, looked at it briefly, then took his stick and began setting type. But about halfway through he paused, mumbled, scratched his beard, crossed his legs one way and then the other. Clearly he was embarrassed. Finally, reluctantly, he took the paper to Greeley's office. "Mr. Greeley, I'm sorry, I don't like to bother you and I know this has never happened before, but I can't quite make out this one word here." Greeley squinted at it, then said: "Why it's plain as day, can't you see? It says..." The old man returned to his stool and set the rest of the editorial, which appeared in the next morning's paper, and nobody, including thousands of readers, noticed anything out of the ordinary. That's according to my grandfather.

Later, when I was nine or ten years old, he would sometimes take me aside when he had finished writing something. He would place two straight chairs from the dining room facing each other, and I would sit in one, he in the other, our knees almost touching. Then he would read to me from the little sheaf of paper with the bold black lines of writing. Manuscript, he called it, and I never forgot the word. He would explain everything to me, all the jokes and allusions, and he would point out especially felicitous passages and read them to me again. And he would ask questions too, he wasn't in the least overbearing or condescending; he would ask me whether I preferred this or that turn of phrase, this or that comparison. He would seem, at least to me, perfectly earnest in his desire for my opinion, as if we were collaborators – an illusion he sustained in other ways as well, often taking me into his confidence. He wrote me letters. He was partial to the comic strip called *Mutt and Jeff*, which had been dropped from his paper in New York, and he gave me the job of clipping it from our local paper (the one my father edited) and mailing the clippings to him in weekly envelopes.

My grandfather's place in Briarcliff was called Journey's End, and on a piece of good paper he had written, in his own hand, "Journey's end in lovers meeting" – from Shakespeare. This was framed, and it hung on the wall of his cabin. The place remained rustic in appearance during my grandfather's lifetime and later. To some extent I think it was modeled, probably consciously, after the cottage at Riverby where John Burroughs lived farther north on the Hudson, the cottage Burroughs described in such books as *Locusts and Wild Honey* and *Squirrels and Other Fur-Bearers*, which I also read when I was a boy. Animals – foxes, bobcats, deer, raccoons, many birds, snakes, etc. – were a part of life around my grandfather's place, and he enjoyed their company and cultivated it. I myself, in Vermont and elsewhere, have tried to create a similar environment for myself, and though I've been forced to it by necessity, at the same time I've made stylistic choices that were influenced by my grandfather's way of life in his last years, choices leading toward an ideal I could never reach, both because I lacked the means – material and emotional – and because it was a product of a child's fantasized view of reality. Journey's End, incidentally, remained in the Carruth family, and my brother Gorton lives there now.

I was eleven years old when my grandfather died. I've no idea when I knew I would become a writer, except that it was well before the age of meaningful self-consciousness, well before I knew what writing meant or had attempted it myself. The notion that I would be a writer was always a fact of my life. During most of my childhood and early youth I thought I would be a newspaperman or a fiction writer or both, like Crane and Hemingway. Although I wrote little poems – scraps of light verse for the school paper or romantic sonnets to exhaust my own adolescent despair – I didn't think of poetry as a potentially serious occupation until much later when I was in my twenties. I didn't even know it *was* a potentially serious occupation, but thought rather it was something that had passed away with the poets my father admired, Rossetti, Bishop Berkeley, Lang, Thomas L. Thomas, etc.

But of course I did become a serious poet and never amounted to much as either a newspaperman or a fiction writer. I don't altogether know why. Often I've wished I had had it in me to be a high-powered political correspondent or a novelist. I didn't. For obscure reasons poetry drew me, practically hauled me off by my coat collar, once I discovered rather late that poetry still existed in the twentieth century and at least some people considered it a feasible, even an honorable, vocation. I was astonished and immensely gratified. Even so, I have always thought of myself as a writer, not just a poet, and in the course of my hack-life I've done about every kind of writing there is (except theatrical writing) ad copy, blurbage, ghosting, magazine filler, direct-mail solicitations, speeches, etc., etc., and I've done many kinds of editing as well. All this because of the impetus my grandfather's example gave me.

The conflict in the Carruth family between Ettie's sternness and narrowness of vision and Hayden's greater receptiveness and expansiveness, whether in city or country, has been handed down to all of us, even to the generation of my own grandchildren. Each Carruth has dealt with it in a different way, often radically different. Each parent has tried to overcome it in his or her children, has tried to right the balances, but never altogether successfully, and in fact often the effort has created only opposite though connecting problems. Who knows? – maybe it all goes back to great-grandfather Oliver and great-grandmother Sarah, the widower and the widow, the rough frontiersman and the righteous matron, who came together as a matter of convenience and threw their children into a mélange of propinquity. My grandfather did marry his sister. The emergency which has been my life is the result of an unnatural but inevitable, though unconsanguineal, incest – way back at the beginning.

My grandfather was a very funny guy. Although his most popular book turned out to be an adventure story for boys that he wrote when he was broke and needed the money, his reputation during most of his life was as a writer of comic stories and sketches in the American frontier tradition of understatement and exaggeration. He was what they called a humorist. Because of him I read the works of American humorists from Washington Irving to James Thurber, scores of them, of whom only a few are still memorable, Artemus Ward, Bill Nye, Petroleum V. Naseby, John Hay, Bret Harte, and of course Mark Twain. Whatever humor I have in my own work derives from them and from my grandfather, as much from his speech as from his writing. Myself, I am no humorist. I have too much neurotic anxiety and pessimism in me for that. But I wish I were. I wish real humor had not passed out of existence, the way I thought poetry had. Maybe it hasn't. Maybe someone will discover a way to be genuinely, singlemindedly funny in our awful time, as my grandfather and his colleagues were in their happier age. I hope so.

A NOTE ABOUT POLITICS should be added to the sketch of my grandfather.

I don't know much about my great-grandfather Oliver, except that he married a widow who owned a gristmill and at one stroke secured for himself a living, a housekeeper, and someone to look after his kids. According to the family genealogy he was born in Lorraine, New York, a hamlet south of Watertown and about five miles from the eastern shore of Lake Ontario (not far from where I live today), and emigrated to Minnesota in about 1860. I was told he did not approve of the Civil War and took no part in it. Does this mean he emigrated to avoid the draft in New York? Possibly. On the other hand his father, William, had emigrated from western Massachusetts to upstate New York in the late eighteenth century, and in fact every generation of Carruths after the original generation in this country, which settled in the Bay Colony in about 1730, moved westward. My grandfather, by moving east, broke the pattern, which is why I was born in Connecticut instead of Montana or Oregon like many of my remote cousins. Some are said to have ended up in Hawaii and New Zealand.

As a young newspaper editor in Dakota my grandfather was a Progressive Republican and Prairie Populist, then in New York a strong supporter of William Jennings Bryan in the 1890s. Later he became a Socialist. He knew Eugene V. Debs, and I've been told he wrote speeches for him during the campaigns of 1908 and 1912, but I don't know if this has been verified. I do know he ran for dogcatcher on the Socialist ticket in North Tarrytown and campaigned by writing waggish, blustery letters-to-the-editor, which no doubt amused his readers but luckily did not get him elected. His four sons, including of course my father, were all Socialists until 1932 when it became apparent that the Socialist Party had become too weak to amount to anything, whereupon like many others they became New Deal Democrats and voted for FDR, only to be increasingly disillusioned during the rest of their lives. They were atheists too, of course, which must have aggravated my grandmother Ettie no end and added to the family's divided personality, all the more since most of them inherited her moralism and austerity without its theological underpinning.

As for me, I read nineteenth-century radical literature when I was in high school. I read it avidly. It fed my depressive sentimental temperament. I took socialism (with a small s) for granted. I can remember plowing through *Das Kapital*, some of Herzen's autobiography, works by or about Blanqui and Fourier, Feuerbach, the Webbs and other Fabians – masses of material, much of it polemical or sophistical (like Shaw's *The Intelligent Woman's Guide to Socialism*), much of it ephemeral and secondhand. I read eagerly and ignorantly and often uncomprehendingly; the stuff was over my head. In general I do not remember having political discussions with my father, at least not many. On the other hand in 1936 when he was editing *The Jeffersonian*, a magazine published by the Democratic party, he took me to campaign headquarters at the Biltmore or the Commodore on election night, the celebration of FDR's tremendous landslide – it was wild. But my clearest memory of that time is discovering a dusty pamphlet in a corner of the local library in Pleasantville, uncataloged and obviously hidden away from ordinary readers. I can't remember its title, and though I think it was written by Louis Adamic I can't find it listed among his works. It described the convention of the First International in Brussels in 1870, the confrontation between Marx and Bakunin, when Marx held out for the proletarian revolutionary takeover of the apparatus of the state and Bakunin insisted that the state was inherently evil and must be abolished. The point was irresolvable. Bakunin and his followers got up and walked out. But in ten minutes of reading and with the force of instantaneous clarity, I was struck by the rightness of Bakunin and the wrongness of Marx. From that point on I've been an anarchist.

When was that point? I think in 1936 or 1937. I didn't say much about it to anyone, except to my friend Johnny Ponturo, with whom I used to roam the streets at night, talking radical politics endlessly. Later, in college, I had political discussions with a few friends, I became a member, or perhaps only a follower (I don't remember), of the American Student Union (the equivalent of the Student Nonviolent Coordinating Committee thirty years later), I attended meetings of the Karl Marx Club, I demonstrated (though I've never been an activist) at protests of the Litvinov-Hitler pact in 1939, etc. My own first book was, in effect, a hundred-page term paper on the life of Wild Bill Heywood, leader of the Western Federation of Miners and the International Workers of the World. I don't remember what course this was for and have no idea what became of the manuscript. When I had a chance to go to New York, which wasn't often in those days cursed with poverty, I'd hang out around Astor Place in the afternoon, the radical bookstores, Tom Mooney Hall where the Communists, Socialists (of various stripes), Trotskyites, Anarchists, and many others would be hammering on one another, and then at night went to hear jazz. I read as much as I could find about the Spanish Civil War and what happened to the Barcelona Anarchists. I was still dreadfully ignorant and without friends who saw politics exactly as I did. It wasn't until years later that I met people whose political evolution had been roughly the same as mine, people like Paul Goodman and George Dennison.

Being an anarchist means inevitably being an idealist and utopian, no matter how one looks at it. At various times I've moved toward social-ist anarchism, cooperativist anarchism, trade-unionist anarchism, and all the rest. But I've never been foolish enough to believe that the abolition of the state could happen in our time or perhaps in any time. Occasionally we used to call ourselves "philosophical anarchists," to in-dicate that we held onto the ideal of anarchism – freedom for everyone – and that our day-to-day, year-to-year political conduct was shaped by that standard even though the mechanics of out-and-out anarchist re-bellion were unfeasible, and I guess that's how I still see myself today.

Because the only fixed principle of anarchism is freedom for all, no ideology, which would require submission, can be tolerated. But one point is worth making in the context of politics today. You can't be an anarchist without being a feminist. One requires the other. I've been a feminist, an advocate not only of women's rights but of women them-selves, since the 1930s, and I was always proud of the fact that the Amer-ican anarchist movement was the first general important political front in this country to be led by a woman – Emma Goldman from Rochester, whom I admired and whose books I read avidly. Other women were important in forming my political and social feeling, Mary Shelley, Beatrice Webb, Margaret Sanger, Jane Addams, Rosa Luxemburg, Eleanor Roosevelt (bless her heart), but Emma Goldman was paramount.

ONCE IN EARLY SPRING, around the first of May, I went up into the woods on Butternut Mountain in back of the Cunninghams to get a start on the year's firewood. I drove my pickup across the meadow, up on the old logging road into the trees, and stopped where the rise begins to steepen. On the right side of the road were some old cherry and yellow birch, big gnarly trees, dead but still mostly sound and good for the woodshed. I knew they were there, and Gerry Cunningham had told me I could cut them. Across the logging road was a small area of young firs, not a thicket exactly, not a clump, but a cluster of them, with snow still two feet deep among them.

However, the sun was warm, the woods were full of moisture, and on the third day I found the carcass of a bobcat beginning to emerge from the snow on the lee side of a small fir about eight or ten feet tall. The cat was perfectly preserved. Probably it had been there all winter, frozen, hidden under the snow. Not a hair was out of place. It was beautiful, lying on its side with its eyes closed, stretched out comfortably as if it were asleep. I didn't touch it. I still don't know how it died. No evidence of a bullet wound or other violence could be seen. Maybe the cat had just been tired, had lain down on a late-November night, had passed away naturally with the new snow falling on him like a quilt. His coat was bright and glossy, tawny and patterned with stripes, soft and thick.

I watched that cat, I went to look at it every day. The second day I could see already that the body had shrunk a little. The eyes were a bit sunken and the whites showed slightly through the slit of withdrawing lids. The coat had lost its shine. On succeeding days the body was not disturbed by anything large enough to disarrange it, but clearly the little scavengers, mostly micro-organic, were at work. It shrunk further, and flattened, still covered perfectly by its coat of dull hair, and I imagined the proceedings within, the gradual but swift evaporation, so to speak, of the flesh, the skin, the sinews, the entrails. This was thirty years ago or more, but even then the wild cats were few. I hadn't seen one for several years. Besides, I love the woods and the creatures that used to inhabit them; I sometimes am overcome by nostalgia for an era I myself never knew, though occasionally I've had glimpses of it – as now with this dead cat. So I looked at it every day, more than once a day, went to it in the intervals of rest when my arms and back ached from swinging the ax and hauling on the chainsaw, and often I stood brooding over it, no doubt making up poems in my head. But I never wrote down any of them.

I don't remember how long it was before the cat was only an old blanket of hair draped over its bones. A couple of weeks, I'd say. Maybe longer. From time to time I'd get a whiff of corruption from it, the dry yet randy smell of death, but it dissipated quickly in the clear cool air of May. I worked in that place for about six weeks. I cut the trees and limbed them, chunked and split the wood, tossed it into the pickup bed, drove out across the meadow to the Swamp Road and home, where I stacked it in the woodshed. I probably got five or six full cords of cherry and hard birch out of that little section, half my year's supply. At some point on a windy day the fur blew away from the cat's remains, leaving its skeleton shining and clean in the sunlight. It was beautiful – so intricate and fine and white on the ground of fallen needles and brown leaves. In fact the whole process of the cat's demolition had seemed beautiful to me.

Why? Usually I'm a little dismayed by the spectacle of nature's implacability. If I find the body of a gutshot deer or a muskrat in a trap, my hens bloody from a raccoon-raid on the henhouse, I turn aside for a moment. But this time I had been altogether unalarmed. I knew I was witnessing what had been a life sinking into the ground, and it seemed to me beautiful, I mean in the fullest awareness of beauty – esthetic as well as moral and psychological. Not sentimental at all; far from it. Of course I don't believe that beauty inheres in nature; it is something we human beings bring with us; it is our manner of perception. Yet the process itself, death and deconstruction there in the woods, perfectly natural and apparently uninfluenced by human needs or appetites, seemed to me to contain all the components of beauty, everything I needed in order to construct my vision of beauty, which was close to my nostalgic vision of the prehuman world. "This is the way I'd like to go myself," I said, feeling for once completely at ease with the idea.

In the end, when I had worked as long as I could afford to in the woods, both in that place and, when the runoff dried, farther up the grade, I took the skull of that cat and gave it to Gerry. "See what I found in your woods," I said to him.

FURTHER ABOUT STAN and the chainsaw. This poem seems to be my most popular. For years now I've used it as the opening poem when I give readings because it always works, it makes people laugh and loosens them up. And I suspect that ninety percent of the hearers think the poem is completely authentic. Even those who may doubt that Stan ever buried the pieces of useless chainsaw probably think that the chair, for instance, was a real chair. But I never saw such a chair in my life. I've seen other old chairs, of course, and I've seen bearskins, and I've used rawhide myself for any number of purposes. But mainly I knew Stan (whose real name was Phil). I knew him well. We were neighbors for twenty years. He and Sadie lived on the other side of the crossroads in a little white house with a barn next to it, and I sat with Phil beside his Round Oak stove many a time, both of us smoking our pipes. Phil used to light his pipe by holding two kitchen matches, one in each hand, against the side of the stove until they ignited, then he put them together and held the flame over the bowl. He got twice as much flame that way, and damn the expense. Which was how he was with everything.

When Phil was younger he worked on the road crew, drove the grader, not only in summer on maintenance jobs but in winter too because they used the grader for snowplowing. Often at night he'd get hungry and he'd go into the market and taste the cheese; if he liked it he'd buy half a pound of it and eat it plain in the cab of the grader while he was plowing the back roads. Not a good idea for a diabetic, but that was his way. He improvised, he did things for himself, he was tough and independent, but he was a slapdash worker. When he wanted to upholster a chair, if he ever did, he'd naturally seize on the closest materials to hand and do the job as quickly as possible. Of course he knew better; he knew he should put grommets in the bearskin and buy some heavy waxed thread or strong cord to use for the fastening. He was as smart as they come. But he didn't bother, he put together the upholstery in a trice, relatively speaking, then sat down in the chair with satisfaction and said, "Good enough. It'll last as long as I do."

A lot of what I knew about the speech of the old-timers in Lamoille County came from Phil. From Marshall too, of course, and from many others. But Phil had a slow, deliberate way of speaking that made the dialect easy to understand, and he was steeped in the old traditions. He was right out of Rowland Robinson. I remember when I first heard him say "dreen" – something about how the beaver pond over beyond Emery's place on the road to Waterville "dreened" into the swamp. I thought he was being idiosyncratic, or perhaps that I wasn't hearing him correctly, but I went home and looked it up in the big dictionary, and there it was, an archaic usage. It taught me to trust my ears, and even more to trust what the people were saying.

In one sense I made up that poem about Stan on the flimsiest grounds. Phil did take over that old McCulloch chainsaw of mine, but I'm pretty sure I didn't sell it to him, I gave it to him. He never buried it, he never drove his Powerwagon through the barn wall, he never reupholstered the chair with a bearskin. But in another sense the poem is authentic: he might have done any of these things. I give myself credit for inventions close to reality, but I couldn't have done it if the reality hadn't been handed to me by the people.

LOUISE BOGAN, WHO WAS a lovely and gracious woman, yet tough as nails and down-to-earth too, used to say: "Never use the passive voice." She insisted on it. In her own work, at least her later work – those wonderful reviews and essays she did for *The New Yorker* – she followed her own prescription. She was the best writer of short book reviews I've ever known. No one today can touch her. Alas, no one today wants to touch her; that old ideal has vanished, has been castigated as "humanistic" or "belletristic" and thrown away. But I admire Louise enormously, for her poetry, for her prose, for her strange and valorous life.

When I first met her it had something to do with the conflict over the Bollingen Prize, after the Library of Congress had awarded it to Ezra Pound in 1948 and stirred up such a hornet's nest as a result. She had been a member of the committee that chose Pound for the prize. I was trying in my ineffectual way to organize a response to Hillyer and Cousins of *The Saturday Review of Literature*, who had attacked the committee viciously, and she invited me to visit her at her apartment on, I think, West 159th Street; at any rate it was near the Manhattan end of the George Washington Bridge. I arrived at the appointed time in late afternoon. She met me at the door, a tall imposing unsmiling woman, let me into her small crowded living room, disappeared into the kitchen and immediately returned with a pint of whiskey, which she plunked down on the coffee table between us. She was dressed in black, very simply. It would have been a frightening and terribly uncomfortable experience for me – and perhaps for her too – without the whiskey. What foresight! What cool! As it was we were on laughing terms in no time. I don't remember what we said, except that it led to a meeting in Princeton a week later with the Tates, Leonie Adams, that fellow whose name I think was Trask, and a couple of others. I do remember that we talked animatedly about many things until dinnertime, when her daughter showed up, a buxom blonde whose name I've forgotten, and by then the whiskey was gone and we all went out to a rousing meal in a neighborhood restaurant.

I always remember her. Whenever I find myself about to write "it is" or "there are," an image of her comes into my mind, literally: her expression could be very stern when she wanted it to be. "Never use the passive voice." Immediately I begin to scramble in my mind for ways to reconstruct my sentence. When I'm reading manuscripts and I find other people using it excessively – as my friend Laughlin does, for instance – I begin automatically to rewrite the other person's text. Yet Louise and I had different ideas about discipline and craft. To her, strict adherence to her rule was a moral imperative, a psychological imperative, something she had to hang onto to keep her sanity in her world, which was clearly insane. To me, the harder discipline, and thus the more productive, is to maintain the tension between principled adherence and intentional, significant deviation. I believe that if one does this well the tension will be stylistically, even morally, apparent to others, effecting a more subtle, more complex rigor than simple inflexibility can achieve.

Sometimes "it is" and "there are" are the most direct and natural way to say what you must say.

I came to be fond of Louise and she of me, though our contacts were limited. I saw her in New York from time to time and once she taught for a semester in Chicago, when I saw her frequently. When I entered Bloomingdale, where she had once been a patient too, she wrote me a beautifully kind and sympathetic letter of encouragement that I kept for

years. Now I don't know where it is. Whenever I read her work I turn
to her poem about the hatch, an extraordinary poem, which shows how
a simple but intense and accurate description of detail can convey feel-
ing in itself. It's an uncharacteristic poem for her because it is written in
long lines and loose rhythms, but she was such a fine writer that she
could use any style successfully. She was a real pro. I believe the poem
was dedicated to Auden.

OFTEN IN RECENT YEARS people – especially my friends in Syracuse
– have urged me to write my "autobiography," by which they mean a
connected narrative with particular attention paid to the women in my
life and to my illness and the means by which I "overcame" it. This, they
say, would be a popular book; it would earn lots of money and be made
into a movie, etc., like the autobiographical books by my colleagues,
Tobias Wolfe and Mary Karr, which have done extremely well, though
I myself prefer Toby's short stories and Mary's poems. Autobiography,
I'm told repeatedly, is the rage, the mode of the era. Maybe it is. I don't
care to read biography of any kind myself, unless the biographee has
been dead for a good long time. But there are a number of considera-
tions:

1. Autobiography without doubt has been the substance of most lit-
erature not only in our time but always. All Lowell did with his *Life
Studies*, his "confessional" poems, was to make explicit what had been
generally understood for generations. Further, though it's all very well
to say, as Zukofsky did, that the part of autobiography the writer puts
into his or her published work is the only part which matters, and that
the rest, the particular details, whether written by the author or by
someone else, is no more than scandal and gossip, at the same time a life
does have a meaning, it may be an important meaning (questions of
importance being essentially inscrutable), and this meaning may not
come forward in the fictions the author has created for purposes quite
other than the explanation of the self. It's not a matter of values, which
I believe are constant in art and reality; it's a matter of varying angles of
vision, resulting in varying degrees and kinds of emphasis.

2. To write about "the women in my life," in the sense this phrase
implies, is an abhorrent notion to me. I know them, at least as they were
at one time, more intimately than anyone else in the world, which is only

what everyone can say about his or her domestic sexual companions. In a sense they have entrusted me with that knowledge, however inadvertently. I won't expose it to satisfy the curiosity of the crowd. That would be not only dishonorable in the conventional sense, which is important to me, but also illegitimate in the procedures of abstract cognition – so I believe. Hence I won't write about these women as they are in themselves, even though they have been deliciously indispensable to me, but only as they impinged on me, only as they were in effect extensions of my own peculiarities, and only as they may be pretty well generalized. By this I mean them no discourtesy whatever but quite the contrary, as I hope is evident.

3. If my life has a meaning apart from its fictionalized aspect in my poems and essays, then my friends are right: the lifelong psychiatric illness and how I dealt with it is crucial. And one of the ways was, indubitably, through women and sex, through love. This was never programmatic, not in the least; yet no regimen could have been more powerful in its application or cogent in its effects.

The important women in my life have been Sara, Eleanore, Molly, Catherine, Rose Marie, Roxanne, Joan, Rachel, Kazuro, Connie, and Joe-Anne. A very few others – like Alice and Susan with whom I did not make love, or Muriel and Helen with whom I did – were important also, especially Susan, but in other ways. Are these their real names? It doesn't matter. Then why not call them A, B, C, etc.? Because that would be *too* much of a generalization, *too* depersonalizing. And how does this list stack up in the mass? I have no idea. I've never read the popular sociological analyses of sexual behavior. I do know that some men and women, including a few of my friends, have had far more adventurous sexual lives than I've had. The fact that I can remember all these names, whether I've fictionalized them or not, would astonish some people. But the truth is that each of these women is someone I've known intimately and intensely over a – what shall I say? – a certain length of time, ranging from perhaps six months (in one case less) to fifteen or sixteen years, it doesn't matter. Again the intimacy and intensity count more than the duration.

I hope the fact of this intimacy and intensity suggests about these women their variety, their differences, their personal selfhoods, their indelibilities. I never in my life picked up a woman casually, I never slept with anyone for less than many times.

Have I been fickle and inconstant? Not in the ordinary sense. I've been monogamous with each of my companions, and I've not been the one who was responsible, directly at least, for the breakups. But in the long term? Yes, of course I've been fickle and inconstant, the record speaks for itself, and I tend to think that fickleness and inconstancy are built into human consciousness inevitably, though how they may function – much or little – in individual cases is statistically unpredictable.

The dimensions of the problem begin to emerge.

HAVING WRITTEN THIS MUCH a couple of days ago, I'm overcome by reluctance. An unyielding inner stoppage that does not articulate itself even in my brooding. I don't know what it is, in spite of all the years of psychotherapy, except that it is profoundly personal and irrational. Is it my anxiety about disclosing the lives of women? But it seems as if I've covered myself pretty well in that respect. It's true I've been a feminist all my life, or at least since I took to anarchism, Emma Goldman's anarchism, in 1935; but my feminist inclination was apparent before then, I'm certain. It was built in, perhaps genetically – who knows about such things? My feelings about women have always been tender and sensitive, by which I don't mean protective, I don't mean condescending, I don't mean patriarchal, not at all. From the first the girls in my class at grammar school – Marjorie St. Pierre, Margaret Shean, Jeanette Curtiss, lovely youngsters who are now white-haired shapeless old women, or in their graves – were closer to me intellectually and emotionally, and by and large much more interesting, than the boys. I don't deny, far from it, a sexual attraction, which at least in my case arose in early childhood, but I didn't then and don't now believe that this necessitates attitudes of domination, idealization, or any of the other behavioral evils which feminists, with good reason, deplore.

Then is my reluctance an anxiety over exposing myself? This is doubtless a possibility, or more than a possibility. Or is it part of the general reluctance that has become more and more conspicuous in my self-contemplation as I've grown into my seventies, a kind of amorphous but, paradoxically, dynamic and operative laziness that prevents me from working or pushes me toward trivial tasks like watching television or answering letters? Is there a reluctance compounded of disillusionment over the futility of one's past and depression over the brevity of one's future that incapacitates many old people, leading them into inaction and silence? I don't know much about geriatrics. But I can't help thinking of Ezra Pound.

This is the turn of the year. We have moved from 1994 into 1995. I've promised myself I will write every day, not letters or recommendations or blurbs, but poems and essays; I shall write for myself, without regard to what other people, meaning publishers, editors, critics, etc., may think. It's a promise I made a month ago when I found, after a year of pain and illness, that I was feeling stronger again, a promise to make my final years worth something, at least to myself, and to avoid the predicament that befell Uncle Ez, even if this means forcing and coercing, a willful effort to produce, which I haven't usually been able to do in the past. So it isn't exactly a "New Year's resolution." I hope it is more than that.

ENOUGH FUFFLING, as my friend Ann Laughlin used to say. The point is that I've never seduced anyone. I couldn't. Psychoneurotic anxiety, which crippled me in my social and professional endeavors, crippled me sexually also – which is only what one would expect. In fact the latter crippling was not only more profound than the former but may have been actually causative or originative, assuming the clinicians can make such fine discriminations. What it means, however, is that all the women I've been with have seduced me. They were needy, in other words. Their needs were great or small and were different in every case, sometimes no more than the simple need for sexual adventure, which is as strong in women, I think, as in men – and why shouldn't it be? But more often the need was a neurotic weakness of one kind or another, a deficiency of ego, and in a couple of cases was decidedly psychotic, schizophrenic – I know I'm using outdated, classically Freudian terminology, going back to my own early experience in therapy, but I don't know the up-to-date jargon. Nor do I intend to go into details, except to say that sometimes these women have been deranged enough to become violent, sometimes they have been merely cross, surly, willful, or otherwise difficult. Because in every case they found that the needs they thought to assuage through me were in fact intractable, or that I, the male lover, was the very one who provoked their needs and angers to begin with – the necessary surrogate for a rotten father or some other male abuser in the past – and thus the last person who could do anything for them, no matter how wise or experienced I might be and no matter how fervently I wished to help.

But the further point, the more important point, is that my needs were greater than theirs. Otherwise I would not have been seducible in the first place, I would not have willingly subjugated my needs to theirs, which is exactly what I did. I did it sometimes for years with the same person, years of extreme distress and turbulence, only to discover – though this usually did not cause the breakup – that I was precisely the irritant, I had been driven into the role established long before by an alcoholic father or an abusive uncle or even a hysterical mother, so that my position, my place, absolutely disqualified me from being helpful. My need to be loved, to be *in love*, to be comforted in my terror and reinforced in my sexuality, was so great that I would put up with almost anything. Which doesn't mean I didn't walk out the door from time to time when the tumult became unbearable for everyone. But I always went back, I was never the one who brought on the final debacle, and when it happened, when the women found how unhelpful I was and took steps to get rid of me, I was always devastated, to such an extent that several times I ended up in personal disaster – in jail, in the hatch, in the emergency room. No one can be blamed for this. My need, like the women's needs, came from far back, I believe in part from beyond the womb, and no one was ever responsible for dispelling it except myself.

At the same time, if there were an easy way, or indeed any way, to mollify a fundamentally inflamed sensibility, the debacles could have been avoided.

One point must be made clear: when I say I was seduced I mean I was not the one to make the first move. Always an unmistakably explicit invitation was extended, and often it was more like a demand. It happens to most men, I'm sure, that they are seized in a passionate embrace when they walk unsuspectingly through a particular door. It happened to me many times. Did I resist? Yes, I did – if I was already well attached to someone else. But if I wasn't, as was the case more often than it should have been, I did not resist at all; quite the contrary. I was a willing seductee, not only with my body but with my mind, heart, and soul, ready to plunge almost instantaneously into desperate, fierce emotional involvement and commitment. In one night, or two, I've given

myself away for the foreseeable future without a qualm. A common
enough case, especially among people of my generation and earlier, for
whom sexual activity means moral activity. We cannot fuck without a
pledge. And I was raised, remember, in a distinctly Victorian culture
even though I wasn't born until 1921, eighteen years after the good
queen died.

So I was always either desperately in or desperately out of love. I was
either happy or miserable. For extended periods I enjoyed the best of
domesticity in word and deed, the best of mutuality, though it eventu-
ally always ended. As I became sexually stronger and more confident, I
also became – without any immodest pretension – a good lover, which
for me means someone who almost, but not quite, entirely devotes him-
self or herself to the companion's pleasure. The delights of the bed were
always supremely important to me. And though it seems paradoxical –
perhaps our clinician can explain it – in my experience angry and in-
secure women are the most passionate and generous lovers...

A YEAR LATER. Yes, we are into 1996. I've been unable to continue this.
I've written other things, a few, poems and bits of prose, but the topic
here defeats me, let the analysts explain it if they can. In summation,
loving, monogamous, and intensely proficient sex has been supremely
important to me in my life. When I've had it I've been happy and pro-
ductive. When I haven't I've been paralyzed by loneliness and alien-
ation. As one says in a dismissive way, I've been sick. What has always
surprised me, over and over again, is that this kind of sex isn't enough
for others, but it isn't. The women I have known have wanted some-
thing more, they have wanted *to be well*. Often I haven't known what
that means, but it meant something – to be healthy, happy, rich, famous,
powerful, brilliant, who knows? And when I've tried to convince them
that wellness is not in the cards for anyone, or for only a few extraordi-
narily fortunate people, and that the recognition and acknowledgment
of this in one's personal life is the only way, paradoxically, to go toward
wellness, I have failed. I don't blame myself for this. Most of these peo-
ple were or had been in psychotherapy, and their doctors hadn't been
able to help them either. All of them were highly literate, they read
books constantly, yet their reading didn't give them the necessary

insight and courage. I think perhaps only religion could have helped most of them, and I was the last person in the world to be able to afford them that.

WHAT NEEDS TO BE ADDED to the above is a note about the present. Many years ago Peter Laderman, who was my doctor at the time (and who has been my friend ever since), asked me what I would write about when the erotic urge gave out. I don't know what I answered, but probably that I'd face that problem when I got to it. Well, here I am – old and sexless. My body has given out, and in some measure my mind too. Yet I am happier than I've ever been, more and better contented. And sex still is important even though I seldom can do what I used to do. My wife is younger than I, a very beautiful woman, and I love to look at her and touch her; we spend a good deal of time being physically together. She is also very different from the other women I've known: more intelligent, more gifted, more experienced in every way, including her experience of sex, including her experience of violently abusive sex. She is much, much wiser. Old age is awful and I hate it; the awareness of debility and deprivation is with me every moment. But I can do nothing about it, beyond registering my disapproval – what I used to call my disacquiescence. I'm lucky, however. I'm not alone, not standing in the checkout line at the supermarket like so many others with my can of tuna and my embittered expression. As I say, in the way that counts most I'm happier than I have ever been, and I know it...

ANOTHER YEAR LATER. It's 1997 now, and I'm preparing this manuscript for publication. In all the foregoing I see my reluctance as if it were a present demon, a specter. And I still don't know how to explain it. It reminds me forcibly of the time in the 1960s when I was living in poverty and an agent from New York came to see me and told me that if I would write pieces about the interesting places I knew in Vermont he could sell them to the high-priced, slick magazines that were popular in those days, *Harper's Bazaar*, *Holiday*, *Life*, etc. I signed a contract with him, which was a mistake. I never was able to produce the kind of pieces he wanted – prose like the frosting on a quaint, old-fashioned cake. Meanwhile he began collecting ten percent of my royalties on the anthology I edited, *The Voice That Is Great Within Us*, simply by virtue of being officially my agent; he had nothing to do with the negotiations that led to the anthology. And he is collecting his ten percent to this day, over a period of more than thirty years, during which the anthology has sold thousands and thousands of copies, far more than any other book I've ever produced. Anyone who thinks I'm not bitter about this should think again. But I raise the question here because the *sensation* of being unable to write what that agent wanted is exactly the same as my reluctance to write about certain aspects of my personal life. It is a mostly mysterious, unexplainable blockage.

WHEN I WAS NINE or ten years old my father gave me a small printing press, a Meriden 8 × 10 platen press with five cases of assorted foundry type, a stick, chase, ink and a roller, rules and leads, wooden furniture, and many other tools and accoutrements: a complete outfit, including an oak cabinet to hold it. I set up the cabinet in the upper hall of the house in Woodbury and went to work. I don't remember everything I printed, but I recall a few poems of my own composition, part of a book about the Arctic – the north being an early and lasting fascination for me – and various commercial or semicommercial jobs, such as tickets for the high school dances, programs for concerts, business cards, and the annual Christmas card for the Carruth family, which was usually made from a drawing by my uncle Max that my father had had photo-engraved at the newspaper shop where he worked in Waterbury.

But the main thing was "The Brownie," a weekly newspaper of my own. I wrote it, edited it, printed it, and sold it to the neighbors for five cents a copy. Since we lived on the outskirts of a very small town and had few neighbors I don't think I ever cleared more than twenty or twenty-five cents for my weekly labors. The paper consisted of one sheet with two columns, a masthead, and a dateline. Probably each edition contained eight or ten paragraphs of "news." I didn't have much type, so the left-hand column would begin at the top in respectable Century, then shift to Caslon, then to Baskerville, and by the time I got to the bottom of the right-hand column I was using script and Gothic faces, which made for a very jumbly appearance. It was the best I could do. We had no money for additional type. My father had obtained the press from a colleague in Waterbury whose name was Mortison and

who was the cartoonist for the paper my father edited. Mort, he was
called. Mort had probably used the press to print some of his own
drawings and had then lost interest, and had sold the press to my father
for very little. Perhaps it was even a gift.

A word about the name of my paper. Brownies were odious little
creatures from a children's book that was popular in that time, or at least
had been popular in former times. I remember nothing about the book
but its appearance, printed in sepia ink on tinted paper with drawings
in the margins of little hominids wearing conical hats and smirking ex-
pressions, tumbling down the pages. I despised them. I despised all the
literature for children I was given to read, from the *Water Babies* to
Alice in Wonderland, all that vapid fantasy – to this day it turns my
stomach. Yet my father thought it was just the thing for a child, and
my mother, perhaps reluctantly, concurred. Such was my relationship
to my parents that I could not, absolutely and necessarily could not, dis-
agree with them, but could only submit. So we had Brownies living in
the cellar, for whom we had to leave a cookie each night before bedtime.
We had Brownies in every aspect of our domestic lives. And when I set
up my press I had no choice but to call it The Brownie Press and to
name my newspaper "The Brownie." How disgusting!

As for Santa Claus, I was expected to sustain my "belief" long
beyond the age when most children are happily disillusioned. In part,
no doubt, this was to protect the sensibilities of my younger brothers,
but why didn't my parents acknowledge this, why didn't they enter with
me into a conscious, companionable conspiracy of benevolent pretense,
as parents normally do? They didn't. I was still professing my "belief"
when I was twelve or thirteen years old, and thoroughly ashamed,
within myself, for doing it. For years I've thought about this, about the
scars on my psyche that have been apparent for seven decades because
of it – and because of many other analogous circumstances of my
childhood. My thinking, my analysis – both with doctors and on my
own – has enlightened me, but the scars are still there and they still hurt.

Yet the experience with the press was beneficial, part of the crazy mix
of influences in my early years. I loved typesetting, I took pains with
makeready and inking, I kept the press and tools clean and properly
stowed. And though never, since then, have I been an active printer, I
have taken an interest in typography, I have admired very much the fine
printers I have known – Carroll Coleman, Barney Taylor of Lewisburg,

Harry Duncan, Tree Swenson, Sam Hamill, Barry Sternlicht, Bob Blesse, and others – and I have always liked to take a hand in the design and production of the books I edited when I was working in publishing offices. I believe that printing is a part of the literary process, an important part. And I know that in the old days, before offset printing and computerized typesetting, printers were among the most literate and intelligent people I encountered – Linotype operators, stone-men, proofreaders, etc. I loved their company and I hung out in press rooms and with the compositors at their machines as much as I could. For years I carried a piece of type – a slug – in my pocket as a talisman.

MY FATHER SHAVED every morning at sunrise when I was a boy, and often I watched him. The bathroom window faced due east. My father always noted where the sun came over the horizon, how it moved from day to day, and he pointed out to me the morning in June when the sun rose in the same place where it had risen yesterday. He *saw* the time when the sun stood still as clearly as did the Hopis when they lined up their kivas with the summer and winter solstices. Seeing is believing. Seeing is being present. Seeing is participating.

THE "HERALD NO. 22A box stove" that I wrote about in my little elegy for Paul G. was similar to other small stoves which were used to heat a single room in the large houses of the well-to-do during the nineteenth century, though perhaps a little larger than most. It was about two feet in length and fifteen inches in width and height; made of cast iron with a hinged door in front – on which the manufacturer's name and the model number were molded in relief – and a small projecting hearth; standing about six inches off the floor on claw-foot cast-iron legs. A good kind of stove, invented in the first place, I imagine, because it was more manageable and efficient than the Franklin stove of the eighteenth century. I bought mine from Frank Church, the junk dealer in Wolcott, for $7.50. It had a crack in one side, which I tried to close with gasket cement, and of course it wasn't made to be airtight like a modern stove, but it worked well enough, at least after I learned the techniques for using it and the patience for putting up with it. I installed it in my cowshed. It wouldn't hold a fire overnight, which meant the cowshed was often −20° when I went out there on winter mornings, my typewriter stiff and clanky, my old electric adding machine frozen solid. I learned to start up a fire quickly with dry kindling, then go for a stroll up the road or back into the house for another cup of coffee while the fire got going. Then I'd put on some larger sticks, leave the draft wide open, the chimney damper also, and let it roar. In an hour or so the cowshed would be warm enough for me to go to work.

At first I rigged up an ordinary tin stovepipe with an elbow that would take it out through the east wall, i.e., toward the brook. This worked, but the pipe rusted quickly from the rain and snow. After three or four years I built a chimney against the north wall with Marshall's help, a good chimney with a poured-concrete footing, a clean-out door at the bottom; it was a structure of cement blocks with a few tiers of brick where the stovepipe came into the chimney (about five feet above ground), and an interior fitted flue of flanged tiles. Fancy. At the top was a granite capstone held up by bricks, and where the stovepipe went through the cowshed wall I had a fine old stone collar, probably talc, that Marshall found somewhere in his immense collection of discarded hardware. The chimney worked splendidly and is still there, as is the stove itself. Rose Marie has turned the cowshed into a little guest house with a porch or balcony facing the brook, very attractive, and though I miss my old cowshed I can't object to what she has done with it, especially since the place is hers now, fair and square.

That stove was a godsend and a great comfort. Oh, I complained about it often enough, especially when the cowshed was too cold or too hot and when I contemplated the soot and ashes that drifted onto my manuscripts and books. But I worked in that cowshed on a good many bitterly cold winter nights, striving to keep a deadline for *Hudson Review* or the *Nation* or somebody; I mean when the temperature was twenty and thrity degrees below zero, and I kept warm. God knows how many trees I fed into that little stove, hundreds I'm sure, maple, ash, beech, birch, elm, butternut, ironwood, apple, willow, even poplar and basswood, anything that would burn (except softwoods, which, like a good New Englander, I consistently eschewed), all reduced to powdery ash. Sometimes on dark winter afternoons when I was depressed and lethargic I would intentionally overheat the stove, then string up my hammock and lie there in semisleep, baking, for hours at a time. It was a luxury such as a poor man could afford, a waste of the time I normally had to husband so rigorously. But now and then such lassitude was a necessary restorative.

What a lot of poetry I wrote sitting in my old oak rocker next to that little stove, with the stovedust sifting down on my head! I'm astonished that I could do it.

MORE ABOUT THE COWSHED. We moved to Vermont in June, and that first summer I worked by the light of a Coleman lamp – a pressurized gasoline lamp with a mantle. The light was more or less okay, but the lamp generated too much heat, and the hissing it made was annoying. In the fall I strung my first wire from the house to the cowshed, by way of the old garage and the old maple near it. I put in an overhead light with a pull-string. It worked well enough. But soon I began improvising improvements, and I wired up a number of outlets, plugged in my old fluorescent desklamp that I had bought years previously in Chicago, then a rickety standing lamp next to the rocker with a shade that Rose Marie made from illustrations cut out of magazines. Meanwhile I had covered all the available wall space with shelves, old boards held up by brackets and wires, and I made an extra little shelf slanting slightly downward for the big dictionary; I put a light above it so I could see the fine print. I built a small table next to the rocker and installed a radio. Eventually I put an air conditioner in the window that faced the house so that I could defeat the summer sun beating on the cowshed roof. And after I built the chimney I installed an exhaust fan (which I took from a worn-out vacuum cleaner) in the old stovepipe hole, because Rose Marie was apprehensive over the immense clouds of tobacco smoke I produced while I was working.

In short I wired up that cowshed like a switchboard. And I jerry-rigged dozens of contraptions to make my work easier and myself more comfortable. Nothing elegant. I was never a good finish-man in carpentry. The shelving was made from used unmatched lumber, unpainted. The woodbox was an old Utica Club crate. The wastepaper was collected in a bushel basket. When I wrote by hand I sat in the rocker, with a piece of plywood resting on the arms of the chair to serve as a lap desk. When I worked at the typewriter I sat on a stool I had made years earlier by cutting the back and dowels from an old captain's chair. Clumps and sheaves of paper were clipped together and suspended from the ceiling on wires and strings. Old photos, postcards, and newspaper clippings were thumbtacked everywhere. It was messy yet orderly; I knew where everything was, my books and files, all my supplies; I could work without the stress of material insufficiency. It was a poor man's shop. Those were the days when I formed the habit of using other people's discarded Xerox paper for all my letters and manuscripts, and I even used the business-reply envelopes from junk mail to send letters to my friends. Because I couldn't afford to buy it, I hoarded paper and never bought any, and I hoarded everything else too: nuts, bolts, nails, toothpicks, old binders, rubber bands, paper clips, bits of pencils and erasers, rusty tools found on the road, crayons, horseshoes, string and wire, everything. I hoarded not just because I'm a pack rat by nature, but because, like my neighbors, I needed these things and couldn't afford to buy them.

What was it like in the cowshed? Another world.

THE TRUTH IS, I was very fond of my cowshed. As much as any poem or essay produced in it, it was my invention. I miss it. I wish it had been properly photographed so that I could see it again.

Adrienne Rich told me once of how she liked to sit on the porch of my house on a summer evening while I was at work, to see the light in the cowshed window, the flowers I had planted, delphiniums and foxgloves and heliotrope along the wall, to hear the brook murmuring, the hens and ducks going to roost, the thrushes and whitethroats making their last calls in the woods.

MY FATHER COULD NOT believe that when Shakespeare wrote:

Golden lads and girls all must
Like chimney sweepers come to dust...

he was making a pun. My father was a literalist, a pragmatist, *and* a Victorian sentimentalist. A peculiar guy, but millions of them existed seventy-five years ago, especially in middle America. The idea that the poet could be making a pun in a serious elegy, or that a pun could be inextricably and meaningfully seriocomic, was alien to everything he believed; it was medieval. And though Shakespeare's pun is so obvious on the face of it that I never questioned it and to this day can't understand how my father questioned it, nevertheless a good deal of the old man's literalism got into me too.

WHEN I WAS IN THE ARMY I wrote my poems in a small round upper room with arrow-slits for windows. The walls were of stone and ancient brick. It was a castle, but nothing fancy, more of a fortress actually, built, we were told, in the eleventh century, located about ten miles north of Cerignola in southern Italy, the region of Apulia. Originally it had been the country estate and escape-house of the local count, who was called the Count of San Francisco if I remember correctly – and I probably don't. He had had a more elaborate castle in Cerignola where he lived most of the time, and the two places were linked by a tunnel, stoned up beautifully and arched for the whole ten miles, so that he could escape when his enemies came looking for him. This was in the flat wheat-growing part of southern Italy, between the Apennines and the Adriatic, perfect for airfields. We had B-24 bases in that area, also bases for B-26s and for the fighter groups (P-38s, P-47s), and I belonged to the 455th Heavy Bombardment Group, which had taken over the count's castle for its headquarters. Originally I had been trained as a cryptographer in the signal branch of the Army Air Corps, but there wasn't much use for encrypted messages in that region at that time. Scrambler telephones had been introduced, and that's how the generals communicated with one another. Hence I was reassigned to the public-relations office. I spent most of the war writing stupid "features" for the newspapers back home, or interviewing GIs on disk for their hometown radio stations. It was dull work. But it gave me the use of an "office" in the old castle, also a typewriter, which I was permitted to use for my own work in the evenings.

Our community had been created almost literally overnight, a small city of tents, huts, shops, offices, remarkably complex. Our outfit, like all the Air Corps, was supposed to be self-sufficient. Our cadre included hundreds and hundreds of specializations, not just mechanics and engineers and flight crews, but intelligence men, historians, even doctors and lawyers. All laid out on that hot plain. We made more dust and mud than had ever been seen in that sector before, I'm sure. And in the evenings, away from the noise and alcohol of the clubs and tents, I sat in the high room, a speck of light shining through the arrow-slit into the darkness.

It was not unlike my shed in the darkness of the Vermont woods twenty years later, another speck of light.

On the other hand when I was in Italy I had no idea what I was doing as a writer. I was ignorant, blind. My favorite poets were Shakespeare and Byron, whose works I had studied as an undergraduate: not bad models in a way, but they didn't prepare me for dealing with my life in 1944. To this day, I resent, bitterly, the inadequacy of my education. I was aware of "free verse" and probably had read a few poems by Carl Sandburg, Amy Lowell, etc., but I didn't care for it. I had heard of James Joyce and *Ulysses* – in fact I'd been told about them by a teacher in high school, Robin Dermody – but had never attempted to investigate them. I had read almost no contemporary poetry or fiction. The only living poet whose work I had read at all extensively was Robert Frost, whom I had encountered in school; a small selection of his work had been published in a "GI edition" by the government, one of the little books intended to fit in a shirt pocket, and I read that with some pleasure, although Frost's conservative backwoodsy attitudes were repellent to me. Otherwise the main reading I recall from that period was *War and Peace*, borrowed from the chaplain. I read it for months, it seems, a few pages at a time.

In poetry, as in everything else at that time, I was bewildered and afraid. The loneliness of my life was acute. I had friends, guys I played poker with and got drunk with, but no one to talk to. I suffered constantly from psychosomatic disorders, including recurrent attacks of "fake appendicitis." Extreme insomnia was the rule. Life had a surreal quality, what I would later recognize as Kafkaesque, filled with a sense of displacement. But in fact this was what I had experienced for years and years, I think ever since I was about six years old. In the army it only became more pronounced.

I wrote sonnets and ballads, bits of comic verse. All gone now, fortunately. I think I did publish a couple of pieces in the *Stars and Stripes*, but I have no memory of what they were. Perhaps I gained a little more skill in versification, which may have helped me later on, but otherwise my writing at that time was of no value at all. Only after the war did I read the poems of Jarrell and Shapiro and McGrath, and see what

I might have done in the army if I had been more aware of the possibilities. As it was, even my letters home were trivial and jejune.

IN THE SPRING OF 1996, when his seventy-fifth birthday was only a few months off, Carruth accepted a schedule of readings and travels that was too much for him. It was a function of his well-known passivity: he always did what anyone wanted him to do. In late February he and his wife spent a week in California, four days at Stanford, where they were put up splendidly in a suite of the Alumni House, followed by two days in Santa Cruz with their friend Adrienne Rich, and a day and a half in San Francisco while they waited for their plane ride home. Carruth was half loaded most of the time, though at Rich's house he stayed comparatively sober; but he did what he had to do, a reading, a seminar, any number of receptions, dinners, parties, and he spent a good deal of time with young people, the Stegner Fellows in poetry and others, who were eager to listen to him. Sometimes it seemed as if they were eager simply to touch him. On the last night in San Francisco, while his wife stayed in the hotel and worked on an application for graduate study that she needed to submit as soon as they reached home, Carruth got fully loaded and was thrown out of a bar or nightclub. Afterward he could not remember its name or location, nor what he had done to provoke the wrath of the proprietors. On the trip home in the cramped airplane he suffered greatly from hangover, akathisia, and joint pain.

In late March Carruth spent a week in Massachusetts, this time without his wife. He did readings at Holy Cross in Worcester and UMass in Amherst, plus constant socializing, both official and unofficial. Again he was half loaded most of the time and fully loaded some of the time. He ended up in Northampton for three days, staying in a friend's house while the friend was away, and there he suffered a breakdown that threw him back into the condition he remembered all too well from forty years earlier, before, during, and after his prolonged hospitalization in White Plains. He was alarmed and depressed, shaking from head to foot. Finally he hired a limousine to take him home. Once there, he sent out a form letter canceling all future engagements, including readings in New York, New Hampshire, and Wisconsin, and asking people not to call him or write to him.

The readings he had given, especially the two in Massachusetts, were among the best he had ever done. The audiences were large. At the end of each reading the people stood and applauded at length, and showered him with very flattering remarks; they bought a good many of his books. Clearly he was a success. But he was also a drunk. He was the last person in the world who could have done such things while he was sober.

Hangovers at age seventy-four, he said, are unbelievably worse than those experienced by the young. For two days in Northampton he did not take a drink, but he was still trembling violently from head to foot, wracked with fear, guilt, and physical pain.

Carruth considered himself lucky to have a home of his own to go to, humble though it was, and someone to share it with him. Otherwise, he knew, he would be in the hospital again. He disliked hospitals and knew that they had never helped him at all in his psychopathological distress.

So he retired, went back again into the sober semireclusion in which he had lived most of his life and written most of his poetry, back again into the old sense of failure and humiliation, knowing that no one could understand his predicament and that many would put it down to some kind of aloofness on his part. He was aware of anger and resentment around him. Most of all he was aware of his own vast disappointment. Without doubt he enjoyed the applause and approval he had received, and he desired nothing more than that his work should be accepted and appreciated. Without doubt his sense of triumphing over his disabilities, even at the expense of drunkenness, was important to him.

FOR FIVE YEARS WHEN he was in his thirties, after he left the hospital, Carruth lived in a house on a side street in an old suburban village next door to the high-school yard, an ordinary but decent house from the last century, three stories high, shingled, with a wraparound porch in front and a small stained-glass window set next to the front door. He lived much of the time on the third floor in a converted attic. He was bothered by loud noises, and when the wind blew hard or the high-school marching band was practicing in the street outside he hid in a far corner of the unconverted part of the attic, crouching and hugging himself. He was loaded with Thorazine during this period, five hundred milligrams a day and sometimes much more, but it didn't help him. He lived at night as much as he could, when the other members of the household were sleeping, so as not to interfere with them, but he joined the others for dinner as long as no guests were present – guests were a serious problem for him – and he tried to do his share of the household chores. Each night at about two o'clock he went out and walked down the sidewalk. Sometimes he walked a hundred feet, sometimes a hundred yards. He had been told that he should walk around the block, but in five years he never made it that far.

It was a painful and peculiar five years.

Carruth had been told by his doctors in the hospital that he would never be able to lead a normal life. He could have caviled with them over "normal," since he was a stickler for the right use of language, but he knew what they meant.

His only friend was the next-door neighbor, who lived in a similar house on the other side of a common driveway, a man he had known for years, a small-businessman, manufacturer of specialty bottles and bottle caps. The friend was an intelligent, kindly guy who read poetry and loved music. One night a week they would get together in the friend's house and play recorder duets, transcriptions of Bach and Mozart. For Carruth this was a great boon, his only human contact outside his family.

Often during this time Carruth compared himself to the crazy aunts or feebleminded uncles he had read about in the gothic fiction of America, shameful relatives hidden away in the dark recesses of some unfortunate family's home.

He played the clarinet for hours every day. He had no music stand, but found that if he placed his open clarinet case on the edge of his bed and propped a copy of Auden's *Age of Anxiety* inside it, this would hold his music at the right level and angle. He played the standard clarinet pieces from the early repertoire, but also more modern things by Hindemith, Berg, Copland, and Milhaud. He had never heard most of this music, so he had to work out the pieces by himself, without accompaniment, and he made many mistakes, especially mistakes of tempo and phrasing, as he discovered in later years. Nevertheless he developed a pure tone and a fair dexterity with his fingers. And of course he spent many hours playing the blues, and learned to improvise freely in five keys.

At one point toward the end of the five years Carruth's next-door friend married an attractive, lively woman of about forty, who had a somewhat disturbed adolescent daughter. The marriage went sour almost immediately. The woman was a good pianist, and she and Carruth sometimes performed together, doing things like the Mozart *Clarinet Quintet in A*, transcribed for a B-flat instrument and with the piano substituting for the strings. She was a good-natured woman with no pretensions, a kindergarten teacher. Once when Carruth was standing at her kitchen door, ready to go back across the driveway to his family's house, she came up to him quickly, embraced him, and kissed him on the mouth in an unmistakably sexual manner. It was sudden and totally unexpected for both of them. It was, in fact, a great gift, or rather a great prize, at least for Carruth, awarded for no reason, out of the blue, by a power whose name and nature were unknown to him. He was astounded. All his hunger sprang into focus immediately. He knew, or unconsciously felt, that in spite of everything he possessed some singular virtue hidden from everyone, even from himself.

And this was the beginning of his thirty-year struggle to reenter the world.

SOMETIMES CARRUTH THOUGHT – almost, it seemed – that the whole country was populated by ex-wives and former lovers. Strange to think of. These women whose bodies he had known as intimately as possible and whose minds he liked to think he had known just as well, out there now in anonymous silence, somewhere – in a few cases he had no idea where. He rarely if ever heard from them. At the same time his best friends were women he had never slept with. Something fundamental, resembling truth, resided in this paradox, though he felt it more clearly than he could articulate it.

He loved these women friends with an affection of enormous power, a compassion amounting to intimacy, and sex had something to do with it too, but the relationships were not sexual. He conversed with these women – by mail, phone, and occasionally face-to-face – in total freedom and candor. And with immense respect, both personal and professional – for all of them were writers. And with tenderness as well, the kind of chivalric concern which he believed lay at the root of the goodness of humanity, and had nothing to do with sexism and all its evils. Instead it had to do with what women and men, in their separate singularity and genderhood, can give to one another, making them truly and significantly equal, truly and significantly different.

For him this difference, the distinction and balance of fe-male-ness, was what brought survival in the midst of metaphysical adversity within the scope of possible human competence.

As he grew older Carruth relied more and more on these few friendships. He could do this because he enjoyed, at home, the remarkable good fortune of a wife who was everything a spouse and lover could be, completely committed and supportive in every way. From his friendships with other women – as, with a difference, from his even fewer friendships with men – he derived a sense of communal understanding and solidarity that made his isolation supportable. And he came to recognize that this had been for him the main factor of carrying on during all his life.

If his friendship with these women was not sexual, then what was it, why was it different from his friendship with men? A difficult question. When he thought about it, what came to his mind immediately was the difference between what a child gets from its mother and what it gets from its father. For good or ill, for whatever reason, a difference between male and female nurturing *exists*. If it cannot be defined, it can be denoted.

FOR CARRUTH THE MOST beautiful thing on earth was not on earth: it was the starry sky at night. As an easterner he seldom saw it, and in his old age, spent in the miasma of upstate New York, almost never. But he remembered the time when he was camping in the Sierras with his son-in-law, Jerome Ward, somewhere a little west of Tahoe. They camped like true foresters, taking nothing with them but tea, a can or two of beans, and their sleeping bags. At night they lay down on the gravel next to a stream where the great conifers opened away and left the sky in evidence from horizon to horizon. Carruth was uncomfortable, the rubble of pebbles and bark on the ground pressed into his back, the sleeping bag constricted him, but he gaped and gawked upward at the brilliant stars in their millions, absolutely spellbound, overwhelmed, until he fell asleep and slept more soundly than he had for years, in peace.

He remembered another time when he and his wife and small son had camped in Arizona on the high desert near Oraibe. He had watched the full moon rise above the horizon spectacularly, orange and huge, seeming so near that it was a personal presence looming next to him, inescapably maternal (though not much connected with his own mother). He remembered the sky above Virginia City where he and his lover walked in the shadowy canyon near the fissure of a bygone mine. He remembered the sky above the plains of Texas, near the Brazos, where he awoke in the morning because a bright redheaded wood-pecker was yammering at him from the top of a nearby pole.

In fact all the most beautiful things of the world were in the west. An easterner born and bred, drawn inevitably by circumstance back to the east, to New England, Carruth nevertheless loved the west and believed it was where he ought to live. The high plateau of the Bighorns, between Sheridan and Gillette, was a place of wonder for him. The mariposa lily was the loveliest wildflower he knew. The coast of Oregon with its huge dunes and extraordinary surf was the seashore par excellence. The long-tailed flycatchers of Texas were the most extraordinary wild birds. The armadillos and golden marmots and grizzly bears were the most interesting animals by far. Even the rattlesnakes and scorpions.

What kind of fate placed him always on drab and crowded eastern clay?

WHEN CARRUTH WAS growing old, becoming an old man, he was as-tonished by the rate of change. He couldn't tell at what point he had moved into unmistakable old age, but he knew he had. He compared himself to others, Stanley Kunitz, for instance, who at ninety was still writing and giving public readings, or Winston Churchill who had smoked maduro Cuban cigars and eaten pie with clotted cream and sipped Courvoisier until he too was ninety, or close to it. Clearly Car-ruth's internal clock was set to a different rhythm; at seventy-five he felt stupid much of the time, physically stupid, a dull sensation in the front of his brain, a heave and gasp at the nothing where words had once been. He couldn't remember the commonest words, like *virtuosity* or *refulgence*, words he had known all his life, so that more and more when he was writing, or trying to write, he relied on the thesaurus in his com-puter – which was not a good one – to tell him what he wanted to say.

Every day was like every other. Often in the morning when he was drinking coffee and smoking cigarettes he would say to himself: "Well, it's a sunny day, for once. This afternoon I'll drive over to Syracuse and see if I can find someone to talk with." But when afternoon came he didn't go. Syracuse, the city he had lived in for a number of years, only thirty-five miles away, an easy hour's drive – yet he realized he hadn't been there for more than six months, and now was unlikely to go again. To the people he had known in Syracuse he had become a creature of oblivion, an unknown presence in the hills. No one knew what he was feeling. No one, as far as he could tell, cared.

Inertia was another word he found in his thesaurus. He recognized the discomfort, slight but evident, that he felt with all words from the scientific vocabulary because his training in science had been so skimpy and he had never had the opportunity, or perhaps the inclination, to educate himself about it, as he had about philosophy, literature, and history. He looked up *inertia* in his desk dictionary. "The property of matter by which it retains its state of rest or its velocity along a straight line so long as it is not acted upon by an external force." Must be something like *torque* in the automobile business. He felt more at ease with mechanics than with physics, though he was incompetent to say what was the difference between them. He remembered a "perpetual motion machine" he had seen when he was a child on one of his family's infrequent visits to New York, a system of ball bearings and hard steel channels: the balls kept rolling round and round, dropping and leaping back up again, in an endless repeated motion with no input of energy to keep them going. It was in the lobby of a bank or some other large commercial enterprise, and he stood and watched it for a long time, fascinated by it, until his parents dragged him away. He knew about friction, he knew that ultimately the "machine" would slow down and come to a halt. He knew that it was merely a curiosity, a gimmick meant to attract public attention, and that part of its fascination was its being a machine that produced nothing, absolutely nothing at all. He felt, even at the age of nine or ten, the metaphysical pull of such a mystery, such a paradigm.

Now, sixty-five years later, no doubt the "machine" had long since run its course and gone to the scrap-heap. He sat in his fat chair with the broken spring in the seat, and he thought about going to Syracuse that afternoon. He knew he wouldn't. He looked for the ten thousandth time at the piles of unread books around him, including new books by his close friends, Denise Levertov, Galway Kinnell, Lynne Sharon Schwartz, many others, and he knew he wouldn't, couldn't, read them. Lionel Rudolph, the doctor in Syracuse whom he greatly admired, had once said to him: "When you hit the steep part of the bell curve of life, changes are accelerated." Yes. He thought about the bell curve – how, when he had been standing in front of the perpetual motion machine sixty-five years ago on the ascending part of the curve, he had been changing just as rapidly as he was now on the descending part, but in the opposite direction, and how at both ends of the curve an individual human being was protected from the damaging impact of change, in youth by amazement, in old age by torpor. Was this a blessing? In fact neither the amazement nor the torpor were enough to keep away one's anxieties, and the idea of a blessing was absurd anyway. Inertia was all. The perpetual motion machine kept going, producing nothing, until it stopped.

CARRUTH LOVED ABANDONED places. In Vermont from time to time he drove up the tortuous, switchback road to the top of Mount Mansfield, or rather to the "chin," as local people called it – because the profile of the crest somewhat resembled a face gazing skyward – where the old hotel still stood, empty for years, a relic of the time when Vermont had been a summer haven for well-to-do tourists who sought the medicinal waters and cool breezes at 4,000 feet. By the time Carruth got there, winter had replaced summer as the tourist season, skiing had replaced golf and picnics in the sun. He stood on the porch of the old hotel, looking away to New Hampshire and Mount Washington, he walked along the old corridors where the wind blew and broken glass crunched under his boots, he stood in the old salon and listened to the vanished tinkle of glassware, scraps of feminine laughter, the long-gone strains of a violin. Something in that place was a solace for him.

Farther down in the valley, near his home, abandoned farmsteads could be found in the woods, many of them. A cellar hole with young birches and poplars growing in it, a well with the remnant of a broken windlass, lilacs and roses in the underbrush. He would sit on the edge of the old cellar wall for long minutes, gazing into the past. He knew one or two old-timers in the village who had lived in these abandoned houses back in the eighties and nineties of the last century, back when the mountain folk were snowed in from November to April or May, back when the trip three miles downhill to the village was a perilous adventure and sometimes ended with a horse foundered and a sleigh over-turned in the snow. He talked to these people, or rather he listened, seriously, avid for news from another time.

In France he visited more than once the eighteenth- or seventeenth-century village on the hilltop near Villeneuve de Berg in the Ardèche, long deserted. He wandered the streets still marked by the ancient walls, he went into houses whose timbers had long since rotted away, he looked through windows where only ghosts still gazed. By the wall of an old corral he could still hear and smell the milling sheep. Somewhere a plaintive musette still sounded a sentimental tune.

At his own house in upstate New York he had the remnant of a barn, the old stone foundation still firm and part of the barn still standing above it though two-thirds of the building was down, the old metal roof flattened on the ground. He could still go inside it, however, into the old horse stable, where the floor was covered with sixty- or seventy-year-old manure, as hard as tiling, and into part of the cow parlor, where perhaps eight or ten cows once lived. From outside, the old building looked weather-beaten, broken-down, but Carruth liked the look of it and did nothing to repair or remove it. The old loft door still swung squeekily in the wind, and he liked the sound. At night the old walls creaked. He studied the old barn often, thinking that if he were a painter he would paint it, if he were a photographer he would photograph it, but always deciding he was glad he was neither of these, glad to let the impression of the ancient barn lie unrecorded except inside his own mind. Sometimes he went and stood in the stable. Once, when he had been drinking, he even slept there on the hard, dusty manure and thought he was at home.

People in the past always seemed enviable to him. What was modern medicine, what was technology, compared to the creativeness of their lives? Warmth and familiarity suffused the world before. He preferred the shady woods to the sunny fields, and when he found a good niche – between an old spruce and a glacial boulder, for instance, or in a hazel thicket – he rejoiced.

DURING MY FIVE DARKEST years, after I got out of the hospital – *ego, auctor, nunc in propria persona* – and when I was living in my parents' house in Pleasantville, New York, years that were dark not only because

of my illness but because of my strained or at least awkward relationship
with my mother and father and because of the detestable milieu of the
suburban village – what kept me going?

Writing was important, of course. Awfully difficult. I used to say to
myself that producing a new line of poetry was like squeezing hardened
glue from a tube – for I was fully aware of just how aggressive and
potentially dangerous the act of writing was – but nevertheless during
those years I wrote most of the poems in my first book, also the long
poem called *Journey to a Known Place*.

Reading was important too, of course, perhaps more important than
writing. During those years of enforced solitude I repaired, at least to
some extent, the defects of my education, reading philosophy – both of
the past and the present – and history and anthropology. I read hun-
dreds and hundreds of books.

Music. Not only playing the clarinet, but listening. I had a somewhat
primitive record player and a radio in my attic room, and the latter
especially was a blessing. I listened to the FM stations from New York.
The jazz program conducted by Nat Hentoff and Gunther Schuller
every week on WBAI was a joy for me, and a constant instruction. It re-
mains the best jazz radio program I've ever heard. But I also became
much attached to baroque European music during that period, and I
listened to Vivaldi, Pergolesi, the Scarlattis, the other Italians, and
especially Buxtehude, Bach, and Handel – also some Mozart, Haydn,
Boccherini, etc. – as much as I could. The Romantics I didn't need;
I'd heard enough of them to last a lifetime as a child in my mother's
house, though in subsequent years I became much interested in late-
nineteenth-century music. I bought a few records, concerti by Vivaldi
particularly, which I played and studied repeatedly.

Loving. I yearned and hungered for Sara, my first wife; I wrote to her
every day, I awaited her visits, when she brought our daughter Martha
to see me, with indescribable longing; I wrote poems for her and little
stories for Martha, I dedicated my first book to Sara (which may have
been an embarrassment to her). Our breakup had been the precipitat-
ing cause of my catastrophe, though Sara was in no way to blame for it:
she did what she had to do. The original causes far predated her. And
all this is another story. Our separation, however, was the principal and
determinative fact of my life, then and later.

Psychotherapy. But this is a poor word to signify what I received from Peter Laderman. Taking account of my years in Chicago and New York, plus my time in the hospital, I had been a patient to six psychiatrists before the term in Pleasantville began. Maybe more; it's hard for me to remember. When I left the hospital I had no doctor, of course, and within a few weeks I knew I needed one. I called a doctor in New York who had been an intern at the hospital, and he recommended Peter, who lived and worked in White Plains, the seat of Westchester County about ten or fifteen miles from Pleasantville. It was the greatest, most important stroke of luck in my life. Peter agreed to see me, he agreed to come to my home – I could hardly believe it. He did. And for five years he continued to do so, every week, an afternoon taken from his schedule, which was a busy one: Peter had a full private practice, he worked one day a week for nothing in the public schools, and on Saturdays he taught at the Columbia Medical School. A most extraordinary person. At first he came to sit with me in my attic room. We talked about my problems, of course, but about other things too, psychiatry in general, politics, art. Peter was (and is) as smart as anyone I've ever known. He had grown up in immigrant poverty in Paterson, New Jersey, and had pushed his way through college and med school with sheer talent and audacity. He was, when I met him, an established and experienced doctor, almost exactly my age. But he was much more; he was the kindest, most generous person I've ever known. After a year of the attic, we began going out in Peter's car, driving around the countryside of northern Westchester, and eventually we stopped in isolated places where I could get out and walk – it was excruciating and I never went more than a hundred paces from the car. Peter, I'm convinced, was the only person in the world who could have explained to me what was happening in terms meaningful to me, and who could have supported and encouraged me to make these unbelievable excursions. I still remember the first time we stopped in a populated place, the main street of the town of Valhalla. Peter parked at the curb. We walked across the sidewalk – across the agora – and into a drugstore, where we stood at the counter and ordered Cokes – myself trembling and gasping, but I did it. The Coke tasted like medicine. It was. But I had made a little journey, a minuscule journey, in the real world among real people, and I had survived. I hadn't fainted or screamed or done anything obscene. I had been noticed by others, and it hadn't killed me. Because annihilation, I knew, was what I had had every right to expect.

Toward the end of the five years I went to Peter in his office on North Main Street in White Plains. I rode up in the elevator, waited in his waiting room, and did the whole thing that I had done in Chicago and New York before the hospital had captured me. I was never comfortable, but again I survived. Then I was invited to go to Norfolk by my friend James Laughlin, and the professional part of my relationship with Peter came to an end. It slid almost immediately into a personal relationship, however. I went to Peter's home on Hemlock Circle, met his wife Lenore – a brilliant woman and a mathematician – and their children, Carol, Steven, and Gerald. When I landed two years later in Vermont, Peter and his family came to visit me, usually once or twice a year when they were vacationing at Forrester's Pond in the extreme northeastern part of the state, and I also went to see them whenever I was in Westchester. Peter continued to counsel me, and sometimes to prescribe drugs for me – once when I was complaining about not feeling well he even listened to my heart and took my blood pressure – but more and more our friendship became a matter of mutual affection. One summer when Peter and Lenore were vacationing on Cape Cod my family and I visited them there, somewhere in or near Wellfleet, I believe, and we all went swimming and ate wonderful fresh flounder and bluefish from the wharf. This was about 1971. At that time Peter was interested in photography and had his own darkroom in the basement of his house in White Plains; I have copies of a number of his photos.

Over the years we saw less of each other, naturally. I finally moved to upstate New York, I broke off most of my other connections with Westchester. But we talked on the phone; Peter continued to give me counsel when I needed it, and for years prescribed Dalmane for me because my family doctor in Oneida refused to let me have it. Peter understood me and my needs better than anyone else could. He had a heart attack in the late 1980s, as a result of which he acquired a pacemaker; a few years later the pacemaker malfunctioned, he had to undergo the difficult surgery again, and then suffered a long recuperation in and out of hospital when a cardiac infection took hold of him. It was an incredibly threatening and painful experience for him, one of the brink-of-death horrors that people in our age of medical super-technology suffer – and then survive, if they do, happily, not to say ecstatically. We are still friends, still in touch. I love to hear his voice on the phone, so warm and reasonable. I send him copies of all my books, not because I expect him to read them, though he does, but because I want him to have them on his shelf as mementos of part of what he has accomplished in his life. Without him they would never have been written.

When I published what was supposed to be my first novel, *Appendix A*, in 1964 – it turned out to be my only novel – I dedicated it to him.

Peter is tall and lanky, dark-complected, slow in movement, quiet and sometimes hesitant in speech. He wears thick-lensed glasses. He has a cat phobia, and when he came to see me in my attic room I used to shut my cat, Tolliver, downstairs. He is a devoted shopper. Once I noticed a big carton of raspberry jam in the kitchen of his house. He had bought it at a discount. He liked to have raspberry jam with his bagel for breakfast, but I thought he had bought enough of it to last the rest of his life. When he came to visit me in Vermont he always went to the retail outlet of the Johnson Woolen Mill on the main street of our town, where he bought shirts – fine shirts, but how many woolen shirts does a person living in White Plains need?

Once, after I had been teaching for a few years, I told Peter I didn't see how any doctor could treat a patient without loving him or her, just as a teacher must love students. "That's right," Peter said.

CARRUTH MAY HAVE BEEN a Luddite – for like most artists of his time (and earlier) he deplored the depersonalizing brutishness of industrial civilization – but this did not prevent him from loving machines. From earliest childhood he had been fascinated. His closest moments with his father had been when, at the end of day, the father answered the boy's endless questions, explaining the principles of fire, water, gears, dynamos, levers, the whole apparatus of mechanics by which human beings augment their puny natural power and speed. Carruth's toys were building blocks, construction kits, model steam engines powered by Sterno-cum-burnt-fingers, crystal radios, and things he made himself, like a crossbow and a static electricity generator. He lived next to the town dump, which was in a cranberry bog down the hill from his house, a source of boundless treasure, old telephones, rusty knives, pulleys and chains. Blacksnakes lived there, the tribe of racers, and once he watched in fascination while a mother snake gave birth to dozens of diminutive replicas of herself, from which he learned the difference between viviparous and oviparous procreation. It all went together, the birth of snakes, the transmission of energy, turbines and pistons, the rotation of the planets. It was all mechanics. It was all fascinating.

Unlike other American boys of his time, however, Carruth had no early experience of cars. His father was a better Luddite than he was; his father detested the automobile and refused to have anything to do with it, saying that trains and trolleys were perfectly adequate means of transportation. So the family never had a car. Carruth understood the principles of driving and when he was in a car he observed the driver closely, but he never drove a car himself until he was in the army in Italy, twenty-one or twenty-two years old. One day in Manfredonia an officer, a stranger, commanded him to drive the two of them to Foggia. Without a word, though with his heart in his mouth, Carruth climbed into the Jeep and drove it to Foggia, with the officer in back. Why? Why didn't he simply tell the officer he didn't know how to drive? A number of reasons.

First, he was abashed by his inability to drive, ashamed to admit it. Second, he was fearful, he was passive, he always did what he was told. And third, he was reckless, some would say fatalistic, he was impelled always by a spark of abandon deep in his personality, which was no doubt what kept him going all his life through one adversity after another, though others couldn't see it. Often enough it got him into trouble.

After the war Carruth drove for a while without a license, but eventually he obtained one from the state of Illinois. His first car was a 1936 Ford sedan, a wreck. He sold it and bought another Ford, a 1942, a wartime car that lacked some of the amenities – no cigarette lighter, no floor carpets – but ran well. He used it in Chicago, back and forth on the Outer Drive to the *Poetry* office, a drive beside the changeable waters of Lake Michigan he never ceased to enjoy; and he drove it to his home in New York and to his wife's home in Alabama. In fact his wife was a more experienced driver than he was, and often she did the driving. In 1951 he bought a new Plymouth coupe. When he moved to New York he found parking so difficult that he gave the Plymouth to his brother. And of course when he went into the hospital and for some years thereafter he had no car, and he let his driver's license lapse. He thought he would never again have a use for it.

By 1959, however, when he was beginning to get out a little, he discovered he had made a mistake. His girlfriend had a new blue Corvair, a neat little car with an air-cooled rear engine; he liked it a lot. Sometimes he drove it. He decided to obtain another license. Taking the test, in White Plains at the state police headquarters, was one of the bravest, most frightening things he ever did, but again his spark of recklessness carried him through: he passed the test and was granted a license. Not long afterward he saw an ad for a used MGA in the local paper, he and his girlfriend went to Hawthorn, a neighboring town, to look at it, and on the spot he bought it – compulsively, recklessly, insanely. He knew nothing about MGs. But the idea of a sports car appealed to him enormously. He paid for the car from the savings he had put aside over the years of doing hackwork and typing manuscripts.

It was a sleek black car with red leather seats and a white racing stripe running the length of it. Knock-off wire wheels. It handled beautifully and had plenty of power for driving on ordinary roads. He loved it. He loved driving at night with the top down, the way he fitted into the driving compartment, sitting on the floor with his legs stretched out straight to reach the pedals, the way the lightly muffled motor reverberated in the dark, the way the woods and fields enclosed him – for he always sought countryside, away from the schlocky suburbs. In the car he felt a kind of security he hadn't known for years. He was hidden, he was away from the unacceptable circumstances of his life, yet he was in control, master of his own destiny – just what he needed. Without the car he probably would never have been able to enter the world again; with the car it was possible, even though his heart was still in his mouth most of the time. Yet he survived a flat tire; he survived the time when unexpectedly he found himself on a huge bridge high above the Hudson; and before long he began driving farther from home, he even drove to Vermont and visited his old friend from Chicago, Wallace Fowlie, in Bennington. When he moved to Norfolk he of course took the car with him and spent many a night driving around the Litchfield Hills.

One thing that was important was the fact that although he was hidden he still was aware of admiring glances from people along the roadside. He was safe, yet people were paying attention to him. He was aware of this, as he was now aware of everything in his life, and he thought about it, the analogy of driving and writing. The car became a paradigm of his own mind.

No matter how shockingly harmful the effects of modern technology are for people and the world, Carruth knew that only technology – the car and the pills he relied on – permitted him to deal with his life and to resume – slowly, slowly – a place in the world.

So he became, in his own way, one of the great American car-loving public. He began learning about cars, reading the manuals, tinkering, and also learning how to drive with the greatest efficiency. He went to the SCCA races at Lime Rock and elsewhere. He bought automotive magazines. For $600 he bought a third-hand MGTD, which he painted bright green and named the Peeper, because when he bought it the peepers were singing. And over the years he owned many other cars, a SAAB, a 1955 Chevy, several American Motors cars, a Fiat, a Colt, and in Vermont he bought an F-150 four-wheel-drive pickup, which he once rebuilt, engine and body, in his backyard, a considerable accomplishment. Later he had an F-250. After he moved to Syracuse he bought, thanks to his salary from the university, a new Toyota Celica, one of the two new cars he ever owned, which was probably his most satisfactory all-around car, reliable, fun to drive, comfortable. He wrote a poem about it. But he never owned a really good car though he longed for one. He rarely even drove a really good car. Once a Mercedes 290, once a Porsche, once a BMW. He thought the most beautiful car ever made was the Ferrari Testa Rosa, and he would have given his eyeteeth to have one.

Two things he taught his son. A love of music and a love of cars.

BACK IN THE 1920S little boys' trousers had no proper fly in them, but rather a small placket in front that closed with a flap of cloth. One time in the schoolyard, when I was in the second or third grade, a group of older boys were picking on me, bedeviling me, as they often did, though at the time I never understood why. The windows of the schoolhouse were open, and girls, a dozen or more, were leaning on the windowsills, gossiping and taking in the scene. They knew all about schoolyard cruelty, of course, and were probably paying no particular attention to me. But then one of the bigger boys got me in a half nelson and bent me backward while he pushed his knee in the small of my back. My little cock popped out in full view of everyone. At once the girls were all pointing at me, giggling, snickering, calling out: "Oops!" and "Jesus, wouldja look at that!" I don't remember what happened next.

Probably I put on a great burst of energy and managed to break away and run like hell. But where would I run to? Home was more than two miles away. Before I got there Mr. Smith, the one-handed constable who was also the truant officer, would have caught up with me in his Model A coupe. Maybe I ran into the basement of the school and hid in the coal bin. I wouldn't be surprised.

What I do remember is my shame and resentment, so abject, fierce, and wrenching. I went back to school, I had no other choice, but I loathed that school, I loathed nearly everything it stood for, and I loathed all schools thereafter too. Yet although this experience – being so exposed and vulnerable – is as clear in my mind as any memory I have, from that day till this I have not mentioned it to anyone.

MY GRANDSON AND NAMESAKE, Hayden Ward, was an impish child to say the least. When he was about two years old, I was visiting in California, and one day in my presence his mother told him to go pee in the pot. With a mischievous smile – no, a wicked grin – he unlimbered himself and peed right there on the living-room carpet. When his mother began to remonstrate, he ran off like a tiger cub. You could practically see him brandishing his tail as he went.

Now, more than a decade later, he has lived through radical displacement – from California to Alabama – and six years of his mother's terminal illness, an obviously very disturbing time. He appears to be a morose boy. He doesn't smile. He spends a good deal of time by himself. But he is intelligent and imaginative, and I predict that although he will have many periods of extreme unhappiness in his life he will also do something unexpected and widely admired in the world.

HUMAN CRUELTY MADE Carruth ill.

Once in the 1920s or early thirties a radio program called *Major Bowes' Amateur Hour* brought his family, like many others, together around the Atwater-Kent in the parlor. It was a contest for amateur performers. The major presided. Winning performances were determined by the applause of the audience. But the major had a little gong, and if someone was performing badly and had no chance of winning, he would bang the gong, interrupting the presentation, sending the person – singer, impersonator, monologist – into embarrassment and withdrawal. At that time a World's Fair was in progress in New York – was it 1932? – in which case Carruth would have been about eleven years old, and the producers of the amateur hour thought they could spice up their program by importing a tribal drummer from one of the African exhibitions at the fair. He understood no English; he was bewildered to find himself so far from home and in such an unlikely predicament. He was no doubt a fine drummer, someone to whom Louis Belson, for instance, would have listened with fascination, but his drumming was meaningless to the audience and to the major. Booing broke out, the major banged his gong repeatedly, relentlessly, but the drummer had no idea what this meant. He kept on drumming until he was forcibly removed from the stage by the major's attendants. And Carruth burst into tears and ran from the room, gasping and retching.

In the whole history this was a minor episode, of course. But Carruth gave his heart to that drummer from Africa once and for all.

The images persist, even now that he is old. Polish farmers, for instance, who are dancing in a field beside the railroad tracks, laughing and making the throat-slitting gesture, as trainloads of Jews pass by on the way to Treblinka. He could understand more easily the existence of individual pathological monsters, twisted and sick, serial killers, organizers of political genocide, the Khans and Hitlers of this world, than he could understand the existence of such brutality in the general population. Hence much of his life was spent in gasping and retching. Call him lily-livered. He captured the moths and wasps that came into his house and released them outdoors. Call him womanish. In the hypothesis of conventional masculine culture, he was indeed more a woman than a man, although he himself gave no credence to such distinctions of gender and had proven his manhood many times over in other ways. He was *glad* to be a woman.

And if his revulsion from cruelty was an effect of his lifelong unfitness and his consequent suffering, so be it. He would not exchange the suffering for admittance to barbarism.

YEARS AGO, WHEN I was a grad student in Chicago, I encountered Kafka for the first time in an avant-garde bookstore on 57th Street. I bought *The Castle*. I took it home and read it, I think in one sitting, absolutely fascinated. Of course I'd never read anything like it before, but the novelty was not what attracted me: the force of it, the incredible mythic rightness of it, was what did that. I reread it, I thought about it, I lived in it. It wasn't like reading *Ulysses* or *The Magic Mountain*, monumental works that inspired me with awe. This was a book I could learn from, a book that touched my own talent and sensibility. And soon I realized that in part the effect of the book was produced by its translators, Edmund and Willa Muir, who did a magnificent piece of work, quite as good, in its way, a Moncrief's translations of Proust. I went on to read Muir's own poems and essays, his autobiography, and found his work greatly to my liking.

Naturally I also went on to read Kafka's other works and whatever I could find about him, Brod's biography, the letters, etc. The first book I read by Paul Goodman was *Kafka's Prayer*; in such a way does one important thing lead to another in literature. But *The Castle*, along with three or four of the short stories, remained the most telling of Kafka's works for me, as they still do. One of the things I learned from it is how unfinishability can be part of the intrinsic moral and esthetic potency of a particular composition. I only wish that my own unfinished works had the same *raison*.

They don't. They are unfinished because I'm too feeble to do the work. The principal one is the epical poem called *American Flats* that I began in 1986 when I came back from Pennsylvania to Syracuse. That's when I bought my first computer because I thought it might help me in writing such a complex and ambitious poem. It didn't. The poem was something I'd been thinking about for years: a full-scale work with four interlocked narratives. The first was the conquest of Mexico by Cortés, told from the point of view of Maria, the native woman who served as his concubine, interpreter, and guide. From reading W. C. Williams's famous essay about Montezuma and Tenochtitlán, and from MacLeish's epic *Conquistadors*, I knew this was the quintessential American theme, and I believed that Maria's was the best, i.e., most dramatic, view of it, the native woman who was in bed with god and betraying her own people. Secondly, I envisioned a love story set in Virginia City, based on my own experience there in 1978, centered on ecological motifs; the name American Flats is from a field and a ruined refinery on the slope of the mountain below Virginia City. Thirdly, a parodic detective story in which all the characters would be taken from the comic strips of the twenties and thirties. Finally, another love story, this one connecting two old people who are living in a nursing home somewhere in the present.

I saw affinities and connections among these stories that would provide plenty of cross-amplification. The work was to be in four books, each book to contain an episode from each narrative, set out in the same order from book to book. The language was to modulate without a signal between poetry and prose and back again. The whole was to be fitted out with interludes and commentaries.

I made a start. I wrote fifty pages or more, reaching into the second book. But that was as far as I could go in the chaos of my life during the late eighties. Today, ten years after I began it, it sits in my computer, in a file marked "Bigdisk," and I know I haven't the energy or mental acuity to go on with it. This is no loss to the world, but how much loss is it to me? I honestly don't know. Sometimes I think it's a good deal of a loss.

IN MY ESSAY ABOUT suicide I wrote that in the aftermath I felt newly connected with the world, able again to perform "acts of virtue." Now ten years have passed, and I've become an old man. I don't go out much. My daily interaction with other people has almost ceased. Am I still connected?

In another essay, years ago, I wrote about the poet in the ecstasy of composition when he – since I am male – is most himself, yet how at that moment he is also most aware of his communion with many others, or with the great Other at the center of humanity. And when the poem is finished and the ecstasy is over, that knowledge of communion still remains. Similarly at the moment of sexual climax one feels utterly at one with one's companion, even though one can have no true awareness of the sensations occurring in the other's mind and body. Then in the morning one embraces one's partner affectionately, and the knowledge of communion is still there.

So it is for the old man in his cave of darkness, regretting his arthritis and impotence and failing imagination. The knowledge of communion is still there.

About the Author

HAYDEN CARRUTH was born in 1921 and for many years lived in northern Vermont. He lives now in upstate New York, where until recently he taught in the Graduate Creative Writing Program at Syracuse University. He has published thirty books, chiefly of poetry, but including also a novel, four books of criticism, and two anthologies. His most recent books are *Scrambled Eggs & Whiskey, Selected Essays & Reviews, Collected Longer Poems, Collected Shorter Poems: 1946–1991*, and *Suicides and Jazzers*. He has been editor of *Poetry*, poetry editor of *Harper's* and for twenty years an advisory editor of *The Hudson Review*. He has received fellowships from the Bollingen Foundation, the Guggenheim Foundation, the National Endowment for the Arts, and a 1995 Lannan Literary Fellowship. He has been presented with the Lenore Marshall Award, the Paterson Poetry Prize, the Vermont Governor's Medal, the Carl Sandburg Award, the Whiting Award, and the Ruth Lily Prize. Carruth won the 1996 National Book Award for *Scrambled Eggs & Whiskey* and his *Collected Shorter Poems: 1946–1991* was nominated for the National Book Award and won the National Book Critics Circle Award in 1992.

BOOK INTERIOR AND BACK COVER design and composition by Valerie Brewster, Scribe Typography. Front cover design by John D. Berry. Both interior and cover are set in Monotype's digital version of Bulmer, originally cut by William Martin in 1790. Martin drew on the earlier English faces Baskerville and Caslon, but gave Bulmer more contrast and narrower width, influences of the "modern" style developing in France and Italy at the end of the eighteenth century. Printed on archival quality Glatfelter Author's Text (acid-free, 85% recycled, 10% post-consumer stock) at McNaughton & Gunn.

OTHER BOOKS BY HAYDEN CARRUTH
AVAILABLE FROM COPPER CANYON PRESS

COPPER CANYON PRESS
P.O. Box 271, Port Townsend, WA 98368
TEL: 360/385-4925 • FAX: 360/385-3985
E-MAIL: cprcanyn@olympus.net • URL: www.ccpress.org